The Teen Code

The Teen Code

How to Talk to Us about Sex, Drugs, and Everything Else—Teenagers Reveal What Works Best

Rhett Godfrey

with Neale S. Godfrey,
the #1 *New York Times* best-selling author
of *Money Doesn't Grow on Trees*

Notice

This book is intended as a reference volume only, not as a medical manual. The information given here is designed to help you make informed decisions about your health. It is not intended as a substitute for any treatment that may have been prescribed by your doctor. If you suspect that you have a medical problem, we urge you to seek competent medical help.

Mention of specific companies, organizations, or authorities in this book does not imply endorsement by the publisher, nor does mention of specific companies, organizations, or authorities imply that they endorse this book.

Internet addresses and telephone numbers given in this book were accurate at the time it went to press.

Printed in the United States of America

Rodale Inc. makes every effort to use acid-free ♾, recycled ♻ paper.

Publisher's Note: The words of the teens and parents quoted in this book have been edited when necessary for clarity, relevance, and space. Some of the people quoted are composites of multiple contributors. Other changes from the original conversations, as transcribed by the authors, were made for spelling and to change the names of individuals for matters of privacy.

Book design by Robin Black, UDG DesignWorks

Library of Congress Cataloging-in-Publication Data

Godfrey, Rhett (Rhett Z.)

The teen code : how to talk to us about sex, drugs, and everything else—teenagers reveal what works best / Rhett Godfrey with Neale S. Godfrey.

p. cm.

ISBN 1–57954–852–0 hardcover

1. Parent and teenager. 2. Communication in the family. I. Godfrey, Neale S. II. Title.

HQ799.15.G63 2004

306.874—dc22 2003028001

Distributed to the book trade by St. Martin's Press

2 4 6 8 10 9 7 5 3 1 hardcover

To my mother.

Writing this book has made one thing apparent to me, you really believe in me. Thank you, for being you.

CONTENTS

ACKNOWLEDGMENTS

First and foremost I have to thank my editor, Lou Cinquino. I promise I'll reimburse you for the psychologist's fees and the Rogaine. But in all sincerity, your patience and sagacity are truly overwhelming; it has been an honor to work with you.

I also have to thank Mitchell Waters. Thank you for believing in a 16 year old, and for making sure he got a kick in the butt when he needed one. I would also like to thank my project editor, Jennifer Reich; cover designer, Tara Long; interior art director, Chris Gaugler; and managing editor, Chris Krogermeier. Your work has been inextricable to the final production of this book.

I also would like to thank all of the experts who contributed to this book: Dr. Judith Waters, Paul H. Yampolsky, Dr. Ruth Peters, Dr. Anthony Gribin, Dr. Ellen Taylor, Dr. Bruce Taylor, and Mary Jane Donnelly. Your insights have been invaluable and have greatly enhanced my work. I would also like to thank Tad Richards, whose experience and wisdom have aided me through this long process.

I also need to thank my teachers, past and present, especially Mr. Pizzo, Mr. Savage, Ms. Sclan, Ms. Cabigas, Mr. Rod, Ms. Lumsby, Mr. Nap, and Doc Burns. Very few can say that they had the opportunity to be taught by those who truly care, who truly love their art, and who are completely dedicated to their students. I am one of those. I have to thank my Head Master, Dr. Dawson. I will never find a problem that you won't have quote for. Without your friendship, guidance, and open door, PCS would have been a very different place.

I also have to thank my sister Kyle. A best friend is not often found so close. To the PCS gang: Hayley, Jason, Katie, Jess, Lucy, Michael, Gabe, Duane, Aly, Graff, Charles, and everyone else I'm sure I forgot, thanks for the material. To Debbie and Corona, I didn't think it was possible to make eating any better. To The Group: Laura and Kristal, my first loves; Dave, my bosom buddy; Trev, mini-tennis and the driveway; Ryan, the Groove Zone; Anthony, sorry about the trampoline; and Maggie, I didn't want the M&M's. I never would have believed I would have friends as amazing as you.

To my family: Aunt Allison, Uncle Irv, Whitney, Aunt Mala, Jason, Dana, Cathy, Dad, Lisa, Nicky, Alexander, and Maxie, thank you for the constant encouragement and support. To Shmuli: I never understood the meaning of the word *godsend* until I met you. You have brought faith into our family and light into our lives. You are truly an amazing person and incredible friend; I could not thank you enough for what you have done for me over the years.

Last but certainly not least, I would like to thank all of the teens I spoke with around the United States for their candor and openness. Without your help this book could have never been realized.

INTRODUCTION

Writing this book has been what you could call a long process. It all started about 3 years ago, when there was a car accident at the end of my street. I, along with all my friends and schoolmates, was rocked by how sudden and tragic it was. I remember sitting in my room a few days after the accident and hearing my mom knock on my door. She came in, sat at the edge of my bed, and tried her best to console me. I have to say it was a gallant effort, but not what I was looking for. If anything our conversation just compounded my feeling of grief. She left not knowing how to help. I sat there, not knowing what I needed or how to ask for it. I spoke to some of my friends about their conversations with their parents. Everyone basically felt the same way I did; the gap between us and our parents was bigger than any of us ever realized.

I asked one of them what his dad could have done differently to help him out. I was expecting him to say nothing, but surprisingly he had a lot to say about ways his father could talk to him. Ways that would make it easier for my friend to really listen and want to open up and discuss things that were important to him. I thought, "Oh, if his dad could only hear this!" And, really, why shouldn't he? What was stopping us from telling our parents our side of things? That got me thinking, and I got set to find out.

Over the course of almost 3 years, I've been exchanging ideas with teens on how parents can communicate with us better. In person, over the phone, and mostly over the Internet, I've talked to kids about their parents, what they have done right, what they haven't done at all, and most importantly, what they could do better. The Internet allowed me to talk with teens from all over the country, in every state. I got lists of e-mail addresses from teenagers I knew. I'd contact them and get more e-mail addresses from kids they knew and on and on, until I had spoken with well over 1,000 teens of almost every race, religion, and socioeconomic level.

I found out quickly that it's not so much what parents say that causes problems, it's how they say it that causes us to shut down, tune out, and stop listening. And I couldn't believe how much of what our parents said was just not getting through. The more I dug into it, the more I realized exactly how much this book was needed. There are so many of us out there who are clueless about drugs, sex, and other potentially life-changing issues, and a lot of teens have gotten in trouble because of it.

I remember I was talking to a few 15-year-old girls

who told me about conversations they had with their parents about sex. They said the entire talk consisted of their parents telling them that sex was something forbidden until marriage. End of conversation. Even if they wanted to obey their parents and understand their views on sex, do you think those girls' questions, fears, and curiosity about sex instantly disappeared when their parents had their "talk" with them? Of course not. They just turned to other places to get answers: real "experts" on the matter . . . other 15-year-olds. But it doesn't have to be like that. I found a lot of parents who were able to get across information on these important topics in a way that showed respect for their teens and, in turn, gain their trust and openness.

Teenagers aren't the only clueless ones. What shocked me most about many of the interviews was how much their parents didn't have a clue as to what their kids were going through. It seems like life has not changed slowly and predictably as it may have between past generations. To me, it looks like our generation skipped a couple steps of normal evolution and jumped right into sufficiently messed up. Every parent I talked to agreed that kids grow up a lot faster these days, but almost none of them understood the extent of it.

At first, I wasn't really sure if teenagers even cared to talk to their parents about this stuff. Didn't they just want their parents to quit bugging them and leave them alone? Even if they did care, were they going to talk to me, a total stranger, about it, knowing that I would be sharing it with parents?

Of course, I got a lot of those teens who just didn't want to talk—to me or their parents. But it turned out that as I went on, for some reason, teen after teen was just opening up to me and pouring out his or her soul about some pretty sensitive topics, and I didn't even know them! (It seems that teens will never pass up a chance to critique their parents on their most important job, parenting.) I heard all about the things that were going wrong in their conversations with their parents—and why, sometimes, against all odds, things went well.

It shocked me as I would talk to some of these teens that their parents *never* spoke to them at all about "the big issues." I think that could be why they were so willing to talk to me.

Yet I kept hearing stories like the one from a teen from New Hampshire. His mom and dad never talked to him about sex or drugs or any other of the "big" conversations because they expected that he should know that stuff by now, between the Information Age we live in and school programs. But guess what? The more information we have access to, the more misinformation we have access to, which you can imagine can cause some trouble. By the way, he was the same person who told me that you can't get a woman pregnant if you have a blood alcohol level over .05 because that is a lethal amount for sperm!

As you will see in the pages that follow, we are living in a very different time, where kids grow up fast but end up in trouble faster. We need our parents now more than ever, but at the same time it seems like it is harder for you to get through to us.

So what did I find out? Why don't parents understand us? Why are parents so clueless to our world? As I put together what teenagers were telling me, it occurred to me that more than ever teens and parents are ending up on different sides of the battlefield. This growing gap created a kind of teen code that parents find difficult to crack. This code does not consist of numbers and symbols and Navajo words; it's actually a lot more complex—it defines how we think and act, why we get tattoos and piercings, why we experiment with dangerous stuff, and how and why we are who we are, teens of today. Consider this book my attempt at trying to help you understand this Teen Code. It's kind of like me going off to spy on the other side to bring you back inside information: the stuff your kids wish you knew. The stuff they wish they could tell you themselves. I'm not asking you to take advice from me. I'm just asking you to listen to your kids. We're only experts in one thing: being teenagers. And I'm hoping that by hearing real teens in their own voices, and hearing what's worked (and not worked) in their families, you'll find stuff that will work in yours.

I also asked my mom, Neale Godfrey, to help out by sharing her thoughts as a parent and as someone who works closely in counseling parents and families in problem solving and financial planning. She spoke with other experts who work with teenagers and parents to suggest a few more ways that you can "crack the code" in your own family situations.

One thing that I have learned from writing this book is a new-found respect for my mother. This one book took me 3 years to write, and I think the other day I found a gray hair. My mom is on book number 14 and still manages to keep her sanity (well, I won't go that far).

I was not looking for—and didn't find—any kind of magic words for you to say to make everything perfect between you and your teenagers. I just wanted parents to understand that it really *is* possible to have good communication with us, as impenetrable as we seem. And it starts with listening.

Chapter 1 DRUGS

Preparation, preparation, preparation. That is really what all talks are for, to prepare us for tough situations that we might or might not encounter and have to handle by ourselves in the future. And as far as tough situations go, drug use—where our decisions could potentially threaten our lives—is pretty high on the list.

The drug talks, like the ones on sex, are what I call the "don't-do-it" talks—because they're the ones where many parents' basic message is just that: "Don't do it." But even here, there may be a difference in some families. With sex, some parents might say, "Don't do it until college, or until a certain age, or until you're married, and then do it in a responsible way," but with drugs the word is more likely to be, "Don't do them *ever*."

The "don't do it" talks can be the most challenging for you and your teenager, and everyone would probably rather just avoid them, but the consequences of *not* talking about the tough topics are much worse than the short-lived discomfort and awkwardness of talking about them. And the hardest things to talk about are also the ones we need your help with the most.

YOU <u>CAN</u> MAKE A DIFFERENCE

Okay, I'm sure you're thinking, "I know I have to talk to my kids about drugs, but will it really make a difference?" I had the same question for teenagers: Can what your parents say—and how they say it—really change the way you think about drugs? The overwhelming answer I heard was "Yes! Well, maybe." Yes, teenagers generally do want to hear what their parents have to say, and maybe because it depends on how their parents talk to them.

Teens were very open about sharing their thoughts with me about things you could do that would make your drug conversations more comfortable and, therefore, more productive. Most important of all, they say that by doing these things, you'll have a better chance of affecting our decision making regarding sex and drugs. (I'll give you their thoughts on alcohol and cigarettes in the next chapter and on sex in chapter 3.)

So, here's the scoop.

"We listen better when you start early."

Drug talks can have different effects at different ages. I'm sure it doesn't come as a surprise that if you can talk to your child before she's experimented with drugs, you will have a better chance to get through to her and influence her decision making. Once she's already begun experimenting with drugs, you have a different challenge: trying to get her to stop, and that's assuming that you even know that she is using drugs in the first place.

For the best chance of having your drug message be effective, start when your kids are young. One thing I've found out from pretty much every discussion I've had with teenagers about this subject: The most successful drug conversations are with younger teens, say 11 to 13 years, and the least successful are with older teens from 16 to 18 (the intermediate ages of 14 and 15 have a great range of success rates). Older teens have already pretty much made up their minds about drugs; either they have tried them or they've decided they're not going to try them. Younger teens are less likely to have experimented with drugs and aren't under the impression that they know everything they will ever need to know about them. Therefore, you have more of a chance of reaching them. But as we all know, age and wisdom do not always go hand in hand. Some teens reach a higher emotional maturity faster than others, so you have to gauge the timing of your conversations. My mom was talking to me about drugs practically when I came out of the womb. I wouldn't recommend delivery room drug conversations as a rule of thumb, but the thing to remember is that younger is better.

I can't remember a time when my parents didn't talk to me about drugs and how bad they are. Some of my friends' parents did the same thing, but it didn't keep them from anything. But not with me—I guess you could say that all that stuff just stuck.

SARAH, AGE 16, FORT COLLINS, COLORADO

I used to rag on Sarah for being a chicken about drugs, but not anymore. I started smoking weed when I was about 14 because I'd heard about it at school, and I thought it sounded fun. I was smoking pretty much a lot for about 6 months, when my mom came in one day, told me to sit down, and said, "I want to talk to you about . . . pot." She said it like she wasn't sure how to pronounce it—it's a three-letter word, how hard can it be! She asked me if I'd ever heard of it, and I said,

"Yeah, I think so, what is it?" It's a good thing I hadn't toked up just before this conversation or I would have laughed myself to death. But lately, I've been thinking Sarah might be right. I see some of my friends who have turned into total burnouts from smoking all the time. I'm thinking I maybe want to ease up a little.

MICHELLE (SARAH'S FRIEND), AGE 16, FORT COLLINS, COLORADO

Is it useless to start talking about drugs if you haven't brought up the topic before your teen is 16? The teens I interviewed said no. While starting the conversations early is best, teenagers of all ages and experience levels told me there *are* ways to get through, to make a difference, and to better prepare your teen for decisions she will face when you're not around.

"We want to hear it from YOU, not just them."

Like a lot of kids, I took DARE (Drug Abuse Resistance Education) in school. This is a program that deals with drug awareness and education; 60 percent of all elementary schools in the United States have instituted DARE in their curriculum to increase drug awareness. This program and others like it are created to inform your kids about drugs and prevent them from experimentation and abuse. This, in theory, is a great thing, but in actuality DARE's effectiveness is extremely limited. Studies have shown that there is no statistically significant difference in drug usage between kids who have gone through the DARE program and those who haven't. Going through the DARE program myself, I was not surprised by this study, but a lot of parents who I told this to were shocked. Now, there are a lot of parents who assume that drug programs like DARE are getting the right message through to their kids about drugs. And some of them think because someone else is giving them this message that they, in turn, don't have to.

Well, it seems as if you do. Teens had a lot of questions and misperceptions about drugs that DARE didn't clear up. And because of poor communication habits between parents and teens, these questions and misinterpretations were not getting correctly cleared up.

> ***What do I think about drugs? Well, heroin and crack and stuff is pretty bad, but pot and LSD and stuff isn't horrible. Look at the 60s—if that stuff was so bad, our parents wouldn't be here right now.***
>
> BART, AGE 17, PALCO, KANSAS

I am not saying that DARE told Bart that LSD is a vitamin, but it seems that sometimes teens hear what they want to hear from their school drug education sessions, and selective hearing concerning such a dangerous topic could have serious repercussions.

> ***What do I think about drugs? Well, I mean everyone knows that Ecstasy is fine—some scientists said it was not bad for you. But I would never touch heroin or any of that other crazy stuff.***
>
> **Dan, age 16, Little Rock, Arkansas**

Not everyone gave responses like Dan and Bart, but the truth is that misconceptions are a very real and dangerous thing, and they're something that you have the power to put a stop to.

It's not that kids think that programs like DARE aren't a good thing. We just seem to get more drug "knowledge" from friends and from TV and movies. As much as we rely on those sources of info, they are probably not the ones that you parents would trust the most to get across the right message about drug use.

And just as there are parents who feel that the responsibility of a drug conversation is lifted off their shoulders because drug awareness programs have done the job for them, there are also parents who feel that their job is finished because kids get all those drug awareness messages on TV. As we all know, the media can sometimes blur issues, and where drugs are concerned, it is extremely important to see things as clearly as possible.

I know a lot about drugs. I see a lot of stuff on TV, and I've seen a lot of movies that have drugs in them, so I would say that I know more than someone who has not seen the kind of things that I have.

GREG, AGE 14, LYONS, ILLINOIS

The truth is that Greg probably does know a lot about drugs from the media, maybe even more than his parents do, but the only way you can really be sure about what messages your teens are getting is to give them those messages yourself.

START RIGHT, END RIGHT

There seem to be a lot of "don't-do-it" conversations that never really get off the ground because parents pick awkward times or methods to bring them up.

I came home from school and sat down at the dinner table, and before I knew it my dad was preaching to me all of the dangers of drugs. I barely had gotten a bite in my mouth.

JOE, AGE 14, OKLAHOMA CITY, OKLAHOMA

This type of approach, where teens feel that their parents have suddenly turned into televangelists, is one of the most common communication problems that I heard about. Joe—and a lot of other teens I have spoken to—told me that this approach feels more like an attack than a conversation. I understand that this is a difficult conversation to have with your teen, and when you finally plan out your words, they can sometimes come out in one big flurry of excitement. But this tactic will make us instantaneously turn off, which I am guessing is quite the opposite of your goal.

> ***I came home from school and began doing homework, when my dad came into my room to say hi. But before he left, he said he wanted to talk about drugs. I thought that he thought I was doing drugs, so I reacted in a defensive way. Then he thought that because I was defending myself about doing drugs, in fact I was. Let's just say the whole thing was a mess. (And by the way, he still thinks I'm some sort of Colombian drug lord.)***
>
> **DANIEL, AGE 17, BOONTON, NEW JERSEY**

You can see how starting a conversation the wrong way can send you off on a path that you probably did not want to travel down. And don't think I'm blaming parents entirely for this; a lot of it is us. We are very sensitive about topics like this, and, therefore, it is very easy for conversations to go sour. We teens seem to be hardwired with certain defensive mechanisms; when we think we are about to be yelled at or lectured, we turn off and stop listening. On the other hand, if you can approach us in a way that makes us feel comfortable, we're all ears. You see, we aren't the brick walls we appear to be sometimes. We aren't impenetrable. For most of us, there are ways in, but there are some important things to remember.

"Pick a place where I feel comfortable."

Sometimes conversations between teens and parents are like a play (except they're all ad lib, they have no intermission for candy and a soda, and they normally have an ending with no resolution). I guess the problem is that most of these conversations end up like a play that you would *never* want to see. But there are some little things you can do that can make a big difference.

To set the scene for a play, any good set designer needs to create an environment that is appropriate for the actions that take place. Without this, a play loses its power. The same goes for your drug conversations. When they occur in the wrong setting, your message can lose its effect. The truth is we listen better when you set up an environment that is compatible with us.

When my dad first talked to me about drugs, we were on a train ride to South Carolina. Of course he started talking to me right when the train pulled out of the station. By the way, that

train ride was 8 hours long. It was horrible—all I did was stare out the window and try to pretend that my dad was white noise. (I don't think that he appreciated it very much.)

Bob, age 13, Miami, Florida

What Bob felt was trapped. He felt trapped in a situation that he could not get out of because he and his dad were in a closed space, and there was no way out for 8 whole hours. Of course, he was right. His dad had planned the conversation for a time when Bob couldn't get away from him. His dad thought that would help; he didn't realize it was the worst thing he could do.

A lot of fellow teens tell me that if the drug conversation happens in a place where they know it will take a small, finite amount of time, their comfort level goes up. It worked for Selena.

The first time my mom tried to talk to me about drugs, she was driving me to school. It was my first week in junior high. She parked the car in front of the school and said "Now, Selena, you're starting a new school and you may be exposed to drugs. . . ."

I, obviously not wanting to have the conversation with my mom, told her that I was going to be late and jumped out of the car.

The next day, she started the conversation when we were about six blocks away from the school. She didn' t lock us into talking about drugs for the whole drive, just a part of it. When we got to school I hopped out, but we'd had a nice little talk, and it was not as bad as I thought.

SELENA, AGE 13, ELLICOTT CITY, MARYLAND

The conversation about drugs can be a tough one, and I realize that the setting where it occurs is a relatively small matter. But sometimes you *should* sweat the small stuff. Even though the setting might seem like a frivolous variable to you, it isn't to us. When teens feel comfortable in their surroundings, they're a lot more likely to open up to you, which will make the conversation much more productive.

"Find a way to jump-start the conversation."

When trying to start a conversation that you know will probably be uncomfortable and unnatural, the worst thing you can do is start off that way. Don't shoot yourself in the foot if you don't have to. So what *do* teens say you can do to get this conversation going? I like to call these "Jumper Cables": segues that help you get your conversation engines ready for action.

Jumper Cables are important because they cut down

on the awkwardness that sometimes accompanies initiating these conversations, and they also will not raise any red flags and make your teen start thinking, "Well, here comes another drug talk." So before you pull out the ol' "So, how about those Yankees? And how about those *drugs,* too?" you might want to think again. (Okay, that might be an extreme example, but you know what I mean.) Something artificial-sounding sets up an artificial air to your conversation and mars your message even before you have a chance to get it out. By using a smooth, natural segue, you set up your conversation so that there are as few awkward moments as possible, getting rid of at least some unneeded discomfort for both you and your teen.

There are two kinds of drug conversations: one where you fuel a discussion brought up by your teen, and another where you initiate the discussion yourself.

When Your Teen Brings Up the Subject There are times when we bring up the topic of drugs and look to you for input. The problem is that we might not be that blatant about it. Maybe we've seen some drugs at school or one of our friends is talking about using. We might not really know the best way to approach you, so we'll drop hints and expect you to pick up on them. We really *do* want to communicate with you, but we need you to pay attention—it takes a good amount of courage to voluntarily talk to a parent about a tough subject like drugs, and if you don't seem willing or able to talk about it, we will give up pretty quickly.

Here's an experience from a good friend of mine.

> ***I told my dad that you were writing a book about communication between parents and teens, and then I told him that you are working on the chapter about drugs. His only response to that was, "You're not doing drugs, are you?" I said, "No, Dad, of course not," and that was where the conversation ended.***
>
> **WILLIS, AGE 16, MENDHAM, NEW JERSEY**

This is a perfect example of a lost opportunity. The father in this situation could have asked a simple question like, "What does he say in his book?" and Willis would have gone on telling him about my research, the information I was getting from other kids, and his feelings about it all. Even a simple "Hmmmm" on the part of the father might have been enough.

Instead of fueling the conversation, he inadvertently cut it off. The thing is, it is a lot easier to have a productive conversation with us if *we* initiate it because those are the times we *want* to talk, or at least we're testing the waters to see if we *can* talk.

I know that Willis (not his real name) isn't a druggie, but he has smoked some pot, and he's done some Ecstasy maybe once or twice. His father doesn't know that, and my friend isn't likely to ever tell him. But I also know that his father missed a good chance to talk to him and maybe get through to him.

When we bring up drugs, we want you to be inquisitive, just not prying. To a teen, being inquisitive means taking the time and having the interest to want to know what we think. Prying is when you make us feel like you don't give a rat's ass what we think; you just want to get the goods on us. And the problem is that there is a fine line between the two.

We like it when you really listen and show us signs that you are really hearing what we're saying. We like it when you respond and ask questions—but not in a way that's obviously trying to find out information to use against us. Basically, just let the conversation flow. You'll be able to find out what you need to find out, and you'll be able to get your own opinions heard because your kid wouldn't have opened up the subject if he didn't want to hear what you thought. But what do you do when your teen does not bring up the subject (which will be most of the time)?

When It's Up to You Of course, not every kid is going to bring up the subject of drugs—and you certainly can't just wait around to find out if your child is going to. So then it's up to you to use your Jumper Cables to initiate the talk. That means finding a segue that makes more sense than "How about those Yankees . . . ?" so that it doesn't come off in an unnatural way.

Here are the types of Jumper Cables that teenagers have told me work best to gain their attention and hold their interest without raising any red flags. Let's start with the most general and nonthreatening ones, and work our way toward ones that are more personal and potentially challenging.

Media coverage. You never have to wait very long to find a jump-starter for a drug discussion in the media (i.e., TV, radio, magazines, newspapers, movies, and music) because, as we all know, the media loves controversy, and drugs = controversy.

> *My mom sits down and watches TV with me a lot. We happened to come across one of those sappy made-for-TV movies. It was one of those after-school specials, and this one focused on drugs. I love watching them because they always turn out to be something like: The kid slips a pill, and then in the next scene is shooting heroine in an alleyway with homeless men and a band of gypsies. Anyway, in the episode the kid takes Ecstasy, and then starts bugging out. My mom asked if that is what actually happens if you take it. We started talking about the ef-*

fects of certain types of drugs, and how the movie was true and false at the same time. It actually was not so bad talking to her.

JENNA, AGE 14, ATHENS, OHIO

The important thing that Jenna's mom did was use the TV show as a smooth and natural conversation starter. This also allowed her to bring up the topic without putting Jenna in a situation where she felt that she had to give out personal information. She kept the conversation in the third person, and she created an atmosphere where she and Jenna could talk comfortably and productively. The great thing about using the media as a conversation jump-starter is that TV comes right into your home and kind of jumps out at you. Also, the media in general can be a source of misperception concerning drugs, and you can use this fact to not only start a conversation but also help us sort fact from fiction.

Religious services. During some religious services, issues that concern the world and the community in general are discussed. Even though drugs themselves will probably not be brought up specifically, topics that you can use to lead into drugs are. For example, a discussion about greed might be the perfect segue into a talk with your teens about the economics of the drug culture, or perhaps about the disregard addicts have for the people in their lives whom their drug use is hurting.

During a church service, the reverend gave a sermon that discussed a passage in the Bible that talks about the body being your soul's temple, and that you must keep it in top form. My mom and I talked about this later on that day and she brought in the aspect of drugs, and how the use of them would go against this passage. I agreed with her for the most part, but I explained to her that some drugs can be used medicinally and that others do not have any long-term effects. We ended up talking for almost an hour about the effects of different drugs on your body, and it wasn't so bad.

PATRICK, AGE 16, MONROE, MAINE

This is just one example of how you can use your religious services as a conversation jump-starter, but if you keep your eyes and ears open you'll be able to find more than you would think. This seems to work best in families that make a regular practice of going out together as a family after the service, for breakfast or lunch, and discussing the sermons. It's always good to find family occasions to talk over important issues. If you do it regularly, then the topic of drugs becomes just one more issue that, of course, you'll talk about.

School programs. In schools around the country, drug prevention courses are being instituted. When parents of the teens that I have talked to got involved in their kids' drug programs, just as they would get involved in their math or English, they could use the information from those programs to start off drug conversations. They are just as important as any other class in school; the only difference is I don't think that your teen could destroy his/her life by getting involved with square roots and parabolas (even if we might tell you that).

I had been taking DARE, a drug awareness program, in school, and my mom asked me if she could see some of my handouts. We would talk about them and discuss the points that they raised. I was surprised because for once we talked about that stuff and I actually was not looking around the room for the nearest window I could jump out of.

BILLIE, AGE 14, WINONA, MINNESOTA

By using a conversation-starter that was not intrusive, Billie's mom created a discussion about drugs that did not make Billie feel like he was even having a drug talk in the first place.

News in your community. We may not follow every local news story, but there are definitely some stories that get our attention—or ones that you'd like us to pay attention to. And since these are real cases, not just TV shows, they make a strong impression on us. Most of us do not walk out of our front door and see a bunch of people doing drugs, but we would be naïve to think that our communities are not touched by drugs in some way. A month ago a kid in my town was busted for selling large amounts of weed. My mom brought it up from the legal standpoint of what "intent to sell" meant (that you didn't actually have to be caught handing the stuff over and somebody handing money back to you to get in trouble with the law). As long as you had enough that it looked like you wanted to sell it, you were still up that proverbial creek that everyone talks about. This caught my interest (I hadn't realized that was how the law was), and eventually we got into a pretty serious conversation about drugs and the law.

Family history. Sometimes, unfortunately, we do not need to look as far away as our community to find examples; sometimes there are perfect ones in our own families.

> *My dad told me about how one of my uncles got into heavy drugs when he was a kid, and during the conversation that uncle was actually there, and both of them got into the conversation. It really interested me hearing my uncle's stories because he made it seem so real, and the stories that started out funny got not funny pretty quick. It scared me that someone so close had a drug problem because I thought they were always somebody else's.*
>
> BENJY, AGE 13, NEW LONDON, CONNECTICUT

Your own experiences with drugs. Now we are really getting on uncertain ground. Sometimes, and I put the emphasis on *sometimes,* teens appreciate that their parents are willing to talk about their own drug experiences, but you really need to analyze your relationship with your teen. I got the widest range of answers to the question, "Would you want your parents to tell you about their own drug experiences?"

My mom and I were talking about drugs when suddenly she started telling me about her experimentations in college. I said, "If it was okay for you to do drugs, why not me?" She said "Times have changed, and anyway I was a lot older." I mean, how can she get all up on me about my experimentations if she herself did the same? And she's right. Times have *changed. Kids grow up a lot faster these days, and we're ready for things earlier.*

MIA, AGE 14, ALBANY, NEW YORK

But I also got responses like this one.

When my mom and I were talking about drugs, she went ahead and told me that she tried pot once or twice. It made me feel tons more comfortable talking to her once I knew that she could relate to what I was feeling.

HANNA, AGE 13, JEFFERSON CITY, MISSOURI

As you can see, confessing your own past drug use may or may not be a good idea. While kids like Hanna may appreciate the honesty, other kids believe that this undermines your authority. One thing I know is that I personally would call my mom a hypocrite if she told me I couldn't smoke weed and then confessed that she had experimented with it in the past.

Some families have found what they consider a safer route. They thought it was important for an adult to talk to their kids about the real-life issues that drug use caused them in their own lives. Rather than having the parent talk about his or her own drug use, they asked a relative, like an uncle or a close trusted friend of the family who had a history of drug abuse, to talk about their stories. The teens I interviewed who had talked to a relative about drug use found that it was a lot easier and had a greater impact to hear real stories of drug use from someone who did not set the rules of conduct around the house.

"Stay away from Hannibal Lecture."

I'm sure that you sat through a lot of lectures from your own parents and teachers back in the day. And you probably didn't like them any more than we do today. And yet kids are telling me loud and clear that they are still getting lectured about drugs instead of having the more productive form of communication: a conversation.

I wonder—when kids feel they are being lectured, do their parents really think they are having a conversation?

> *My mom and I were having a talk about drugs, or shall I say* my mom *was having a talk about drugs. The whole time I could not get one word in, she was basically just talking to herself.*
>
> KEISHA, AGE 12, PALO ALTO, CALIFORNIA

If all that you are doing is talking *at* your teens and not talking *with* your teens, there's a good chance they'll feel like they're being lectured—because by definition, they are. If we think we're really involved in a dialogue, we'll talk. If we think it's a rant, we tune parents out. This might sound like a weird analogy, but hang in there with me: If you are trying to get an animal to trust you, a common technique is to get on the ground and put your head at its level so it does not feel intimidated. Once you are at its level, you are no longer such a threatening presence, and it gives the animal a feeling of comfort. You almost need to do the same thing with your teenager; you need to get on his level. When you talk *at*—or worse, *down to*—us, we feel like you are imposing your authority on us. You're creating a gap between you and us, and causing us to feel like we can't open up and talk. But when you talk *with* us as a partner in conversation, it puts us on the same plane, and just like a cat or dog we'll feel much more comfortable, and you'll have a better chance at having us exchange our honest ideas and opinions. Of course, as a parent, you are in a place of authority, but it's maybe not the best time to remind us when you are trying to start a conversation.

To be honest, I've seen a lot of teenagers talk down to their parents, too. And you know what that does—gets the parent even more upset and frustrated with their "know-it-all" kid. Sometimes when we act that way, we are really just trying to overcompensate for being talked down to by our own parents for so long. Or we are trying to take advantage of what we see as weakness, or our parents' lack of attention to our teenage life. In any case, my point is that if either side is refusing to be open to true conversation, not much is going to get accomplished. Even if you think it's your kid's fault, as the adult it's still your responsibility to try to fix it. Nobody wants to have poor communication with his or her parents, but if we're not willing to try to fix it, you have to.

"It's nothing personal."

When things get personal, we get nervous.

My dad I were having a drug conversation when he asked me point-blank if I was smoking weed. Of course right away I said no, but then he persisted and asked if any of my friends

smoked weed. Stupidly, I told him that I was not going to tell him that. The whole thing turned into one big fight.

RICKY, AGE 14, CEDAR FALLS, IOWA

This is one of the most often repeated mistakes I hear parents are making during their drug conversations. It surprised me at first, but not after I kept hearing it over and over. Was Ricky's dad expecting him to say, "Yes, Dad, I do smoke weed, tons of it; in fact, I have some with me now. Would you like to smoke?"

I know it's what parents, most of all, want to know, and I don't blame you. But you know as well as I do what will happen if you come on too aggressively in trying to find out. Personalization is the one surefire way to destroy any attempt at having a productive drug conversation. It shows us that you really don't care to have a real talk with us; all you want is to get the goods on us (a message I am guessing that you do not want to convey).

When you personalize and ask questions directed at your teen, it immediately puts her on the defensive because anything she says could be incriminating. Personalization gets you absolutely nowhere; You stand to destroy the conversation and still not really find out about whether your kids are doing drugs. It's like a verbal kamikaze mission. Nothing gets accomplished and chances are you will crash and burn.

I'd say that 99 percent of the time if you ask any question that is pointed at your teen with the intent of trying to get her to incriminate herself, the answer that you will hear back will be a resounding "NO," and I'm just being generous. There may be one out of a hundred kids who'd say yes, but I've never met them or heard of them.

There is this anti-drug commercial on TV that says if you want to know if your kid is doing drugs, just ask. This could not be any further from the truth. Think about it like this: You are at an airport about to go on a vacation, and that attendant behind the desk asks you if you have packed your own bags. Just before you blurt out your preset answer, you remember that your friend put a little present in your bag as a surprise and told you not to open it till you get to Aruba. You know darn well it's harmless, but if you tell that airline attendant the truth you will be brought into a room, your bag will get ripped apart, and, if you are lucky, Olga will give you the best body search you've ever had. Or you can say no and be on your way without incident.

If any of you are thinking that you would tell that attendant that you did not pack your own bag, well, then, Olga is waiting. But for the other 99.9 percent of you, chances are you're not about to interfere with your vacation plans by reciting unneeded information that will get you in a sticky situation.

Kids see personalized questions in the same way. No matter how often you lecture your kids about always telling the truth, you know that everyone—child or adult—won't always tell it, or at least won't volunteer all of it on certain occasions. Even if your kid is basically honest, he's not going to want to tell the truth to a question like that and throw himself under the bus for no reason. Personalization is a pointless and counterproductive tactic.

There is one more form of personalization that some parents don't really realize is personalization at all: asking us questions about our friends.

> ***The other day I was having a drug conversation with my parents when my dad asked me if my friends did drugs, and he named specific people. For the rest of the conversation, I had to defend the fact that my friends were not drug addicts.***
>
> **Jocelyn, age 16, Menomonie, Wisconsin**

Asking questions about our friends will get a reaction from us that is no different than when you ask us a question about us. If we tell you that a friend of ours does drugs, we think you'll probably assume that we do too.

Kids told me that when their parents start asking personal questions about their lives or their friends, what started out as a conversation (or even a lecture) quickly breaks down into a courtroom drama, with them playing the role of defendant and their parents being the prosecutors. If your goal is to make your teen feel like she is on trial, then personalization is the way to go, but if that's not what you want, then you need to look for other ways to find out what you need to know about your child's behavior.

One effective technique that came up from my discussions with kids was when their parents talked about a situation in the third person. Keeping your conversation in third person will allow your teen to discuss his feelings on issues without feeling like he'd better watch what he says because you're prying into his life. So, instead of, "Did you do drugs at that party last night?," the parent asked, "What kind of drugs do people do at parties?" This allows us to let you know what we are seeing without putting ourselves on the hot seat. To avoid personalization, teens told me that their parents avoided words like "you" and replaced them with general words like "teens" or "people." This way they could get the information that they needed without pointing any fingers.

"Don't try to scare me with your stories."

I can't tell you how many times adults have told me stories about when they were teenagers and all of the crazy stuff that they did. Most of these stories end with a shake of the head, a small, gleeful, reminiscent laugh, followed by words like, "I can't believe I ever did that."

Let's face it, the reason why you can't believe you ever did those things is simply that you aren't a teenager anymore. At the time, it probably seemed like a great idea. I guess that's the scary part for you. You know things do get kind of crazy during the teenage years. We go through puberty, growth spurts, pimples, lankiness, clumsiness, and the list goes on. But during all of this there is a lot of activity going on somewhere else: in our brains. I always hear parents saying that they feel like their teens are disconnected. Well, you're right, but in more ways than you would have imagined. Some of the neurons in our brain actually disconnect and reroute themselves to the "adult configuration" during our teen years. Parents can't believe the things that they did when they were teens because—literally—the wiring in their brains was different!

I call this classic teenage craziness with no regard for consequence the "Superman Syndrome." It's where we feel we are unstoppable, that nothing can hurt us or affect us. And I know that it is your worst nightmare when you think about this syndrome mixed with the dangers of drugs.

What I have found is that a lot of parents try to counteract the arrogance that goes along with the Superman Syndrome by using scare tactics in their drug conversations.

My parents told me a story about a group of teenagers who went blind from taking LSD and staring directly into the sun for too long. I went on the Internet and found out that this is an old urban legend from back in the 1960s. It never happened, but some guy made it up because he wanted to scare hippies.

SASHA, AGE 16, MECHANICSVILLE, PENNSYLVANIA

Sasha's parents probably didn't even know the story was made up—they just wanted to scare Sasha into realizing drugs can make people do things that are harmful to themselves. In this case it clearly backfired, and for all we know she now may come to the conclusion that if that *didn't* happen, then LSD may be okay after all. But true stories can be just as bad if they're so wild and unusual that your child can't possibly believe they could happen to her. Scare tactics do have a tendency to work for a short time, especially on younger kids, but teens told me that their effect wears off when new information from friends starts to take their place.

The scenario I heard most often goes something like this: Parents tell their kids a story about a kid smoking weed, and then about something terrible happening because of it—say being permanently brain damaged for the rest of his life. They believe their parents without question and repeat the story to their friends. But as they get older, they hear stories from other friends and acquaintances about marijuana that do not end up with someone in an insane asylum. Most likely they just hear stories about kids having a good time. So eventually they disregard the scare-tactic story and think of it as false because they now have had an overwhelming amount of evidence against it from people they've come to trust. By then, parents are right back where they started (and maybe even further behind) because there is a good chance that the kid will think that any other story that resembles the original one will also be false.

"You're not going to do drugs, right?" is not a conversation.

Here's the most common drug conversation kids have told me about: the classic line that they get right before they're about to walk out the door to go to a party.

"You're not going to do drugs, right?"

I feel this is a less-than-useless thing to say. The answer is just as much of a cliché: "Of course I won't." It seems like part of a script that millions of teens and parents play out every day.

Every time I go hang out with friends my mom asks me if I am going to be doing drugs. Of course I say no. I think that she is

just trying to make herself feel better by saying that because it does nothing for me. And even if I was going to do drugs, does she think that what she said would change anything?

BENNY, AGE 15, CHESTER, NEW JERSEY

If you've had *real* drug conversations with your kids, you should not feel like you need to keep asking this question every time your teen leaves the house. I understand that there is an urge for affirmation, to have a sense of peace that when your teen leaves the house he will not do anything wrong. But the many teens that I have interviewed feel that this cookie-cutter dialogue is just a substitute for having real conversation.

"If drugs are so bad, why do people do them?"

Especially with younger kids, there is much confusion about why people do drugs in the first place. It makes no sense that, hearing all of this information about how bad drugs are and all of the negative effects that they have on your body, that anyone would actually want to use them. So kids know, or soon learn, that they aren't getting the whole story.

Then we grow up, find it out for ourselves, and think we've stumbled on some great secret that you obviously don't know about. It's the revelation of, "Wow, *now* I know why people do drugs" (or maybe that was the revelation of

Woodstock). When you focus only on the negatives about something, you look only at one side of the story. With all of the slanted views on drugs given to us by the media and society itself, it's up to you to tell the whole truth.

When I asked teens what their parents told them about drugs, they were almost 100 percent one-sided accounts. Now I'm not saying you should tell your teen stories of your fun drug experiences in the 1960s and 1970s, but it is important to give a more balanced perspective. One response from a teen that I interviewed made perfect sense.

> *My mom said that some drugs make you feel happy, but it's not real. And that many times when you are not on the drug, not only are your problems still there, but they can be worse.*
>
> PENELOPEE, AGE 13, FRANKFORD, DELAWARE

Telling us the reasons why drugs are so attractive, coupled with their destructive effects, will show us that you are willing to give us a more balanced picture, and allow us to feel that it is easier to be more honest and open with you.

"Tell me something I don't already know."

This is where an important part of your preparation comes in. If you're not going to tell your kids urban legends about blind pot smokers in the loony bin, what are you going to tell them?

Kids know (or think they know) quite a bit about drugs, so you may want to do your homework first. This way, you'll be prepared to talk about different kinds of drugs, the "highs" that they give, and what they're actually doing to your body. The thing is, you don't need to make up scary stories about the harmful effects of drugs. The facts themselves are scary enough to make an impression on your teenager.

The kids I surveyed told me that they became suspicious when their parents just talked about "drugs" in general, as if every drug were the same. Again, this makes us think/realize we know more about drugs than you do. There are all kinds of substances that are more or less powerful, more or less easy to get hold of, more or less expensive, and more or less common around your kids' schools. They don't all make people feel the same way, and they don't all have the same effect on our systems.

Weed, speed, hash, salvia, Ecstasy, peyote, coke, E, K, acid, 'shrooms, heroin, crystal meth, opium, LSD, crack, crank, ice, wet, angel dust, and PCP are just a few of the drugs out there, and I have not even gone into prescription drugs. This might seem a little overwhelming, and the truth is, it is. But that goes back to the preparation part. Before you can prepare your kids for the world, you've got to prepare yourself and brush up on your drug knowledge.

Of course, drugs have changed a lot since the 1960s and '70s. We're in the era of designer drugs, drugs that are chemically created in laboratories, and a whole lot of other drugs that most parents have never even heard of (or maybe they know the names, but no more than that). Knowing about today's drugs shows us that you know what you're talking about and might just get our attention.

"Guess where I am getting my drugs . . . from YOU!!!"

Most of us have had to use prescription drugs for one thing or another, but we use them because they are prescribed to us by a medical professional. But lately abuse of prescription drugs has been on the rise, especially with teens. Why? First of all, they are easy to find. You might be shocked to find out that your kid may not be buying her drugs from the dealer on the corner—that she is getting more than she needs from *your* medicine cabinet.

> ***My dad broke his leg in three places in an accident at work and was given a painkiller called codeine by his doctor. I had heard that if you take it when you are not hurt that the effect is pretty cool. I really liked it, so I kept taking pills from him for months***

until his leg healed. But now I just bum pills from my friends, who take them from their *parents.*

JOSH, AGE 17, DARWIN, CALIFORNIA

This happens under the nose of tons of parents every day and they are totally oblivious. The fact is, many teens are obtaining prescription drugs undetected—because the drugs themselves are not illegal, they don't cause any red flags to go up. But it goes further than this. Not only are pills taken, they are also sold to other kids. The buying and selling of prescription drugs in school is an increasingly widespread practice. You should just see the frenzy for focus-enhancing drugs like Adderall and Ritalin around finals and midterms. There is big business to be had for the kids who are actually prescribed these drugs.

While teens might not know the exact dangers of different types of street drugs, for the most part, they know that they definitely don't have *positive* long-term effects. But do teens know the dangers of prescription drugs? According to most of my interviews, the answer is no.

I have been taking prescription drugs for a while. But I would never take any real *drugs. If a doctor gives those pills to people, how bad can they be?*

CARY, AGE 16, RANDLETT, OKLAHOMA

Well, the answer is a lot worse than some would think. Some drugs can be harmful if taken incorrectly. Also, people cannot take certain types of prescription drugs when they have certain pre-existing physical conditions—not to mention allergies. All of which are reasons a trained medical doctor is the *only* person who can and *should* prescribe you medication. But this fact gets ignored by most of the teens that I have talked to because the majority of users think the same way Cary does.

What, if anything, can you do to prevent your teen from using prescription drugs? Teens say a few things. One piece of good news I have found through my interviews is that you don't have to change the dynamic of your basic anti-drug conversation. Teens told me that when their parents used the tactics that I explained early in this chapter for street drugs, the conversations about prescription drugs were just as productive. There were two main points that seemed to have the most effect on us and that would probably be good to bring up. One is that the idea that all prescription drugs are safe is false, and the other is that prescription drugs can be just as addictive and harmful to your body as illegal drugs. For a lot of teens this information will come as a surprise. Not only will this show your kids that you know more than they think, it will also make them think twice before taking a drug that they thought of as harmless before. But there is one aspect of prescription drugs that is more difficult to handle than the rest.

"I thought I needed it to help me concentrate."

The scary truth is that with some prescription drugs like the performance/focus-enhancing drugs like Adderall and Ritalin, there is a good chance that you will never know if your child is taking them or not. This is a frightening realization, but it's true. Most of the usage of these drugs is in a school environment, and only someone who is begging to be caught would even attempt to use a drug in school that would be even remotely noticeable. I don't mean to keep dropping bombs, but the continued usage of these types of drugs, in some situations, is unintentionally encouraged by none other than *you*.

> *For my entire high school career I was what you would call a good student. But the workload of junior year was getting to be too much for me, and my grades were starting to slip. A friend of mine was prescribed Adderall for ADD, and she offered me a pill so I could concentrate better, get more work done, and have more energy. Well, she was right: The stuff was great, I did more work than I had ever done, and my grades were better than ever. But it got to the point where I would need to take so much to get the same effect that I would have so much energy at night that I could not sleep. Then I would have to take more pills just to function normally the next day. This vicious cycle would go on and on, and I would eventually crash by the end of the week and*

sleep most of the weekend. I was going to stop because of this, but I didn't, mainly because my parents and teachers were so happy about my school performance, and they wanted more than ever for me to get into a top college. So I kept taking pills until I graduated and got into one of those great colleges (which of course everyone was so proud I got into). Then when I got there, things went downhill. I stopped taking Adderall because I realized that the hard part was over and done with: I finished high school and got into the college that I wanted to. But when I was off it, I felt like I was stupid in class, and slower; I just didn't feel like me. I ended up leaving halfway through my first semester because I couldn't take it.

KRISTAL, AGE 19, RARDEN, OHIO

I am not saying that if you commend good grades then you are probably causing your child to become dependent on performance-enhancing drugs, and I am also not saying that you should be suspicious if your teen's grades start to rise. Even though you will probably not know if they are taking those kinds of drugs, there are still some things that you can do that will make a big difference. But before you can do those things, you need to understand that times have changed drastically in the scholastic world. Back when you were applying to schools, things were not *nearly* as competitive as they are today. There is so much pressure on us to succeed that sometimes we feel that we cannot handle it all. When I interviewed teens whose parents understood this fact, they were able to help alleviate some of the stress that causes teens to turn to performance-enhancing drugs. They explained to their teens that they knew how they felt, and that if they needed any help in school, like tutors or a lighter workload, that they would just have to ask. But by all means, I am not saying that you should *not* encourage your kid to get good grades. I am saying that when you let them realize that you understand that these are tough times, and that you are there if they need any help, you open a new outlet to your kids other than drugs: you. Sometimes we need a kick in the butt to get back on the right track, but setting yourself up as someone who is there to support and help, rather than nag and pressure, can make a bigger difference than you would think.

IF YOUR TEEN ACTS SUSPICIOUS

First of all, may I give you a word of caution? Don't jump to conclusions too quickly. I've been mistakenly accused of doing drugs twice, so I can tell you what it's like.

The first time was when my friend's mom saw me, my best friend Dave, and my cousin Trevor outside on the lawn. Our backs were turned to her, and unfortunately, she saw smoke and heard us laughing, so she automatically thought we were smoking weed. She called my mom, Dave's mom, and Trevor's mom; everyone went nuts.

What we were doing, which would have been easy enough to prove if someone had just walked over to take a look instead of all the mom-calling, was this: We were lighting matches and burning leaves on the ground. Call me crazy, but I don't think it is an oddity when friends laugh together, with or without the presence of smoke.

The second time I was accused of doing drugs was when I was very tired one morning and decided to buy a vial of ginseng. Does it work? Is it just one of those health-food fads? I don't know, but it's legal, and you can get it at any health-food store. Anyway, during the school day I was fiddling with the bottle and I peeled off the label. The next day my mom confronted me in the kitchen after she found the vial in my laundry. By the time I got home from school the theories about the mysterious vial had gotten out of hand. Not only was I told that I was shooting up heroin, I was also told that I must be in some type of South American drug ring. Of course this was all news to me, and when I heard it I could not help but laugh. (Somehow, my mom didn't think it was nearly as funny as I did.)

False alarms can send two messages. One is that I'd better be careful what I do because my parents have me under the flame (no pun intended). The other is that my parents are psychos and they obviously don't trust me, so I better watch what I say around them.

The first message may actually be helpful, to a certain extent. If teens know that they are being watched, some may be more hesitant about doing something wrong. But along with that hesitance can come the reluctance to talk to you about anything drug related because they think you are already suspicious of them (which you are).

The second message makes us think that you are morons (which you want to watch out for because teens reach that conclusion very quickly) and that you're making wild accusations because you know nothing about drugs, and more importantly, nothing about us. It also sends a message to your teens that they are treading on conversational thin ice concerning drugs. This almost inevitably will destroy the chance for any future drug conversations (your teen won't even ask you for a bowl for his cereal in fear that you will have him in drug rehab within the hour, assuming you know what a bowl is in drug parlance).

Accusing your teen of doing drugs is a very serious thing. Before you actually do it, try to know for sure. Do your research on telltale signs of drug problems and abuse. Web sites are good for this research. Or you can take a seminar on recognizing drug abuse. There are plenty of sources for this information, and my mom provides some pretty good advice in her section of this chapter, but remember that if you see some of these signs in isolation they might not mean anything at all. It is a much better indicator of a drug abuse problem when the signs are seen together.

As you know, the teen years are a whirlwind of activity. Our bodies and minds are going through a huge and sometimes awkward transformation that takes us on an emotional roller coaster of ups, downs, and pitfalls that eventually spits us out in a place called adulthood. We unwillingly get torn away from the comforting blanket of youth and are forced into a new and frightening world that has to be faced head on. We have no control over this transition; it is happening *to* us and there is nothing that we can do about it. At such a tumultuous time, it's easy for teens to turn to drugs in an attempt to look cool, fit in, or just escape reality for a while. To make matters worse, drugs are more complicated, stronger, and easier to get than ever. And we're getting mixed messages from friends, movies, school, and maybe even our parents about how to decide what to do.

This is why your help is so important. As much as we may never admit it, we need you. I guess you know that or you wouldn't be reading this book in the first place. Drugs are a scary reality that touches all generations and that seems ready to envelop ours. But talking with us may have the power to stop this. By listening to the voices of teens, you are discovering how to break down the stubborn and defensive walls that adolescence seems to automatically build in us and to give us the knowledge that will keep us safe in this unsafe world.

Cracking the Code:

A Mom's View on What a Parent Can Do

No, no, no. That's any parent's answer to the question of drugs. And wouldn't it be wonderful if it were that simple? We just say no; they just don't do it. But the truth is, it's not. According to the American Academy of Child and Adolescent Psychiatry (AACAP), "most teenagers will have some experience with alcohol and drugs. Most will experiment and stop, or continue to use casually without significant problems. Some will use regularly, with varying degrees of physical, emotional, and social problems. Some will develop chemical dependency and be destructive to themselves and others for many years. Some will die, and some will cause others to die."

Okay, that about covers it. Do you have chills running up your spine yet? I do. Especially because I know all of us are focusing on the end of that list: Some will die, and some will cause others to die. We're afraid our teenagers are focusing on the beginning part: use casually without significant problems. If we could hide the first part so that no teenager would ever see it and just broadcast the last part, we would. But we can't, so our job is to make sure that they see the whole picture and how devastating the potential consequences are. We need to make them understand that the game isn't worth the risk.

The conversations that Rhett had with kids across America were very interesting. They're teens, they think they know better than their parents about everything—especially about these life-threatening, addictive, mind-ruining substances that we call drugs. So it's not easy for parents to make these "talks" work, as Rhett universally found out from his respondents.

As parents, nothing frustrates us more than a teen's "know-it-all" attitude. But in the case of drugs, this attitude is particularly dangerous. To protect their kids, parents need all the information they can get. You really do need to know more about drugs than your teens do. And if you're like many parents, you don't know enough.

"Don't make a mistake, because a mistake will get you the disrespect of your kids," warns Judith Waters, Ph.D., professor of psychology at Fairleigh Dickinson University in Madison, New Jersey. She stresses the importance of knowledge above all. "Learn the stuff. Don't go in there riding your horse, carrying your banner, and criticizing. Read everything you can get your hands on, and know what you're talking about."

Here are a few of the things you need to know.

What drugs are out there. We know about marijuana, heroin, cocaine, and LSD. But these days, those are only the tip of the iceberg. The National Institute on Drug Abuse also lists club drugs, inhalants, MDMA (Ecstasy), methamphetamines, PCP, prescription medications, and steroids as potential threats to your teenager. Make sure you know what all of these drugs do, and what their symptoms are.

What drugs are in your neighborhood. Drug fads come and go. Club drugs and designer drugs come and go. If your kids will talk to you about what they've heard on the street, that's great. But there are other people who'll know: The local police will know; school guidance counselors may know.

It's good to get a network of parents involved through a school or civic group, or even through a group of concerned parents who know each other. Invite a police representative or a school guidance counselor to speak to your group, and hold a question-and-answer session.

Use the Internet as a learning tool, too. The Web site of the National Institute on Drug Abuse (www.nida.nih.gov) has a lot of information on drug programs and on specific drugs. A Google search under *drug awareness [your state]* will yield a wide range of local resources.

What drugs do. What are the effects on the body and mind of different drugs? For example, "Ecstasy creates particularly poor judgment in terms of sexual relationships," says Dr. Waters. "Everything starts feeling warm and fuzzy, and suddenly someone you've known for 7 minutes becomes a wonderful, serious relationship."

Make it your business to find out the specific effects and dangers of different kinds of drugs, especially the drugs that may be making the rounds in your neighborhood.

And remember, as much as your kids know about drugs—or think they know—there is one thing they don't know, and that they can never know: what it is that they're actually taking. For example, anabolic steroids are sometimes prescribed by doctors for certain very specific physical conditions. Teens—mostly boys, but an increasing number of girls—use them to "bulk up," to develop muscles, or to look more "buff." But many kids don't know that the average dose of "street" steroids is likely to be 100 times more powerful than the average prescribed dose.

What's in that pot, that acid, that Ecstasy? Is it laced with strychnine? Is it cut with baby powder or some other placebo, or is it incredibly strong? How does it interact with alcohol, or with other drugs?

Recently, we were at the hospital visiting a friend when two teenagers were brought in. The kids who were with me knew them slightly. They'd done a drug that was being passed around at a party. Snorted it. It turned out to be pure morphine. These were bright kids, from an Ivy League college. One came in with a sheet over his head. He hadn't survived the ambulance trip. The other, we discovered later, had permanent brain damage.

"We'd never be dumb enough to take anything like that," the kids with me said.

"How do you know?" I asked. "How would you know what it was that you were taking at a party? When someone says, 'Try some of this, it's great stuff,' how do you know what it is?" Make sure your kids understand that there's no quality control when it comes to street drugs.

How to recognize the signs of drug abuse. It's important for parents to realize that some teens are more "at risk" than others to develop substance abuse problems. You do have to talk to every single teen about the dangers of drugs—and do so often and powerfully—but you also need to be aware that kids who come from families with a history of substance abuse, kids who suffer from depression or low self-esteem, and kids who feel they don't "fit in" anywhere need extra special attention. All teens are going to feel to some extent that they don't fit in; that's natural. But you need to be concerned when that feeling becomes chronic. Dr. Waters told me that there are only two reasons people use drugs: one is to feel good, and the other is to feel better. The most at-risk kids are the ones who need to feel better.

As helpful as Rhett's fieldwork is, there are some things that kids just won't deal with, and this is one. Rhett's friends say don't personalize—don't ask what I'm doing, don't talk about what my friends are doing. I know from experience that this can seem like a dead end. One of your kids' friends is found in a coma with a needle in her arm, rushed to the hospital, put into rehab, gets out . . . and then it happens again. You mention this in a conversation with your own teen, and immediately it's "Problem? What problem? She doesn't have a problem. Anyone can make a mistake or two." Well, even if your kids aren't going to admit there's a problem, you know there is, and you know that one way or another, you have to be very much on the alert for at-risk behavior.

One way or another—and you know what? I take Rhett's research, and his conclusions, very seriously. I've learned a lot from what he's found out, and from his own insights. But while there are some times you have to bite your tongue, there are times when you have to follow your gut and call dangerous, out-of-control behavior exactly what it is. Will your teen shut down and stop listening to you? Maybe. But those parental words can be like ants at a picnic. You squash most of them, but still some of them get through.

We need to talk, and talk in a useful way. We also need to watch, and watch carefully. The warning signs may be subtle, and we may not want to see them. But we really have no choice. Here are some things to look for.

- Physical symptoms. Does your child have trouble getting out of bed? Not just the normal teen-sleeping-in syndrome because she stayed up playing the guitar all night (and because teens really do have a metabolism drop in the morning). I'm talking about real lasting fatigue and lethargy. Is your child sick a lot? Does she constantly have a red, runny nose; glazed-over eyes; a nagging cough?

  These symptoms don't always add up to substance abuse, but they certainly warrant a trip to the doctor, whether your teen wants to go or not. In fact, a trip to the doctor without warning may be an even better idea—for a complete checkup that includes drug testing. Okay, it's high-handed, and it may cause a fight. But you have to find out.

- Emotional symptoms. We're told to watch out for sudden mood changes, irritability, irresponsible behavior, despondency, self-esteem issues, poor judgment, bouts of depression, lack of concern for others, a general lack of interest, and withdrawal from family and friends.

  If you're a parent of a teen, you're now saying, "Yes, and your point is . . . ?" We know all too well that all of this falls under the category of typical teenage behavior.

  The point is, you need to notice *changes* in behavior, and pay attention to them.

- School issues. Watch out for a sudden drop in grades, a lot of absences, or general discipline problems. Again, it may be time for that sudden trip to the doctor. According to Dr. Waters, this is one of the best signs of substance abuse.

- Social problems. Here, you have two very different points of view. The AACAP warns to watch out for "new friends who are less interested in standard home and school activities, problems with the law, and changes to less conventional styles in dress and music."

Rhett reported this a little differently. "Here are some things that you probably don't have to worry about because they are perfectly normal: Your teen dresses in a gothic or wild way. Don't assume that your kid is a drug addict just because he has blue hair. Clothing, hair, and piercings are a normal teen outlet," according to the kids he spoke with.

Who's right? I say, pay attention to both pieces of advice. Don't jump to negative conclusions about your child, but don't wear rose-colored glasses, either. Dr. Waters talked about this, too. You risk coming off like a jerk for overreacting to the fact that your teen suddenly starts wearing white pancake makeup and a dog collar? Well, Dr. Waters points out, "There are worse things than being a jerk." It's the lot in life of parents, anyway. See what's behind the sudden change in behavior.

All of this revolves around very tough judgment calls. The classic warning signs of substance abuse (except for the chronic health problems) may just be classic warning signs that you have a teenager in the house. But they also can indicate real trouble, especially if they occur suddenly. If you're unsure, don't make the diagnosis yourself: Consult experts, doctors, psychiatrists, psychologists, drug counselors, school counselors—anyone who might be able to help. Your family physician or pediatrician should be the first stop.

And one more thought: The two kids who had overdosed on morphine made a more powerful impression on the kids I was with than anything any parent could say. I don't recommend hanging around emergency rooms with your kids, waiting for a friend to be brought in. But I do recommend encouraging your kids to volunteer for crisis hotlines, suicide hotlines, or drug abuse hotlines. Let them hear the stories, firsthand, of kids who are at the end of their tether.

Chapter 2

ALCOHOL AND CIGARETTES

Most adults would define cigarettes and alcohol as drugs. Most teens don't.

You see, we teens have constantly run into some incongruencies with good ol' Merriam-Webster. As you probably have already noticed, teen vernacular seems to differ from yours. Sometimes it's just that we use a different word for the same thing. (You say "making out," we say "hooking up"; you say something is "OK," we say it's "chill.") But when it comes to alcohol and cigarettes, it's kind of the opposite—we use the same words but have different meanings. So when you hear "alcohol," you think "drug." When we hear "alcohol," we think "no big deal." And it's the same with cigarettes.

The dictionary calls a drug "something, often an illegal substance, that causes addiction, habituation, or a marked change in consciousness." So that would mean cigarettes and alcohol would be considered drugs, right?

Well, teens have their own definitions. We think of the social aspects of a substance, not its medical effects. Not what it is or what it does to you, so much as how people use it. "Drug" always has a negative connotation as something that's socially rejected, so alcohol and cigarettes can't be drugs—they are socially embraced. No one really wants to admit to doing drugs—drugs are bad! That much we know. But everybody drinks and smokes, so those can't be bad. They can't be drugs. I've found, from the teens I've talked to, that many parents accept this definition, too.

My mom's not stupid. She knows that kids drink and smoke, and she knows I do, too. It's not like she likes me to do it, but it's also not like she tries to stop me.

MARYANNE, AGE 16, OTWAY, OHIO

I'm a senior in high school, so of course I drink and smoke sometimes. My dad is pretty cool with it, we just have a rule that I can never drink and drive. Sometimes when I have parties at the house with a few of my friends he'll buy us a couple

thirties and take everyone's keys; he knows that stuff is no big deal.

TOM, AGE 18, CYPRESS, CALIFORNIA

Many parents seem to accept the effects of drinking and smoking. If you think about it, as much as most parents would not like their kids to drink and smoke, they still don't seem to put drinking and smoking in the same category as drugs. A lot of the kids I've interviewed have parents who would go through the ceiling if they thought their kids were doing drugs, but they at least accept the concept that drinking and smoking are normal outlets for adolescents in general. I guess this is probably because parents are more familiar with alcohol and cigarettes and maybe consumed them when they were teenagers themselves.

I'm not saying that most parents allow their kids, or should allow their kids, to do these things, I am just saying most teens report their parents realize they're *going* to try these things. (That's very different than most parents' views about their teens using drugs.) And you know what? They're right. According to the Centers for Disease Control and Prevention, Youth Risk Behavior Surveys, and the American Cancer Society, seven out of ten teens have tried smoking cigarettes, and eight out of ten have tried alcohol. You see, as much as you are trying to convince your kids to not drink or smoke, the whole world is telling us a very different story. Every time you turn on the TV or catch a glimpse of a billboard, you're sure to see at least one gorgeous, barely dressed woman holding a beer between her two perfectly full, red lips. Sound enticing enough? On top of this, we see people drinking and smoking almost every day and frequently find ourselves in situations where we're able to do the same. Since you can't (a) take down every billboard of voluptuous beer-swilling twins; (b) bring back Prohibition; (c) stop movie stars from smoking in the summer's hot movies; or (d) implant a camera into your teen's forehead to catch his every action, you're stuck with (e) find the best way to talk to your teen to help him make good decisions on his own.

A lot of the same things from the drugs chapter about timing, Jumper Cables, and keeping it third person apply in this chapter—and the next one, too. But each of the "don't-do-it" talks have their own subtle differences.

WHAT WE'RE THINKING

Here's what the hundreds of teens I've talked with think you should know when you talk to them about alcohol and cigarettes.

"Just because you don't give it to us, don't think we can't get it."

My mom tells me that I can never drink for the rest of my life. Yeah, right, like that is going to happen. I'm not saying I'm going to be some sort of a wino, but it's stupid to think that I'm not going to drink once in a while.

JASON, AGE 15, NEW ROCHELLE, NEW YORK

My dad is really strict on me; he makes sure I "keep myself out of trouble." He never lets me drink even a sip of wine, and he would have a heart attack if he saw me with a cigarette in my mouth. But whenever I go to parties or hang out with my friends, I can drink and smoke as much as I want and he has no clue.

NALLOU, AGE 15, HARRISBURG, PENNSYLVANIA

I know for sure that my parents don't want me to drink and smoke, but it's not like they can do anything to stop me. If I want to drink, I can; if I want to smoke, I will; and if I don't, I won't.

JEROME, AGE 16, BLAINE, WASHINGTON

I don't do any bad drugs, I just drink and smoke some pot. It's not like it is hard to get some booze, but the funny thing is, it's a lot harder for me to get a beer than to score an eighth of herb.

KATIE, AGE 14, MANASSAS, VIRGINIA

We all find ways to do the things that we shouldn't, and teens are as crafty as they come. A teen can get *whatever* he wants *whenever* he wants if he has a connection and money (the latter of the two being the only hard one to acquire). Unless your teen is John Travolta in *The Boy in the Plastic Bubble,* you can't monitor his every movement and keep him from drinking or smoking. The thing is, Katie is right: Legality makes cigarettes and alcohol harder to buy, but in reality, "harder" is just a short step away from ridiculously easy. A teen looking almost of age can buy both with even a semi-realistic fake ID, which one can acquire for about $50, and those teens who could never pass for the legal age either have friends who do or have more inventive ways of getting what they want.

My friend and I stand outside liquor stores and give people money to buy us stuff. Normally they say no, but there'll always be some chill guy that will buy us whatever we want if we throw in a few extra bucks for him. We get cigarettes the same way; it's just too easy.

TOM, AGE 14, ALBERT LEA, MINNESOTA

My grandma smokes, so whenever I go to her house I take a few packs from her carton. It's not like she'll know the difference.

KARI, AGE 12, KENNEDALE, TEXAS

My mother and father don't drink so they don't keep any alcohol around the house, but I have a lot of friends who have parents that do. So when I go over to their houses, I bring a water bottle and ask them if I can take some. It depends on who it is, but normally they let me.

GANDEE, AGE 15, LANCASTER, PENNSYLVANIA

Laws for the most part do not deter us from drinking or smoking, they just force us to be craftier with our methods of attainment. This is important because it seems from my interviews that some parents do not talk to their teens at all about cigarettes or alcohol; they assume that their teens will not be exposed to them until they are of legal age, and by that time they'll know how to handle them responsibly. But as we have just found out, this could not be any further from reality. There is certainly truth in the saying, "Ignorance is bliss," but when we are discussing substances such as cigarettes and alcohol, both of which can have detrimental effects on your health and life, a new saying fits into place: "Ignorance is risk." The risk of misinterpretation.

"It can't be as bad as you say it is."

Drinking is not bad for you; I just read a study that said if you have like a couple glasses of wine a day that your heart beats better. And they also found that the hops and stuff in beer also does something good for your system.

LEA, AGE 13, GILBERT, ARIZONA

Smoking can' t be as bad as everyone says it is. I know a whole lot of people who smoke and have nothing wrong with them.

JOHN, AGE 12, KAMUELA, HAWAII

Drinking hard stuff like vodka and whiskey will mess you up, but if you have a few beers or some glasses of wine, you' ll be okay.

DACY, AGE 14, MIDWAY PARK, NORTH CAROLINA

If you have a few drinks and then you drink tons of water and pee a lot, they' re gone from your system in like an hour.

BRETT, AGE 15, TULSA, OKLAHOMA

It would seem from many of my interviews that there are a lot of misconceptions about drinking and smoking. These misconceptions can come from many sources, from the romanticized version of them in the media to even personal experience, but the thing to remember is that having the wrong idea about alcohol and cigarettes can lead you down a dangerous path.

Dacy thinks that a shot is different than a glass of wine or a beer. Dacy could run into real trouble thinking she really isn't that drunk after having a few beers and a glass of wine—in actuality she just had the equivalent of four shots. Brett's misconception could get him in just as much trouble. Even if he drank bottle after bottle of water, nothing will get that alcohol out of his system other than the time it takes his body to absorb it.

SO WHAT WORKS?

Talking with your kids about smoking and drinking can be a tricky task. Many of us feel more than uncomfortable talking to our parents about anything of substance, let alone actual substances. The placement, time, and conversation initiators can make or break the productivity of your conversations, and since alcohol and cigarettes cause the death of hundreds of thousands every year, it is important to make sure you get your point through. As I conducted my interviews, I asked teens things like: Where would be the best place to have a conversation about cigarettes and alcohol? What would be the most comfortable way for your parents to start off a conversation?

I went on and on like this, asking teens about all of the beginning aspects of a productive conversation. Everything from timing and placement to lecturing and conversation initiators was very similar to what teens told me before, in the drug chapter.

I guess this makes sense because cigarettes and alcohol *are* drugs, even if most teens don't think they are. But even though teens say the best way to begin a conversation about smoking and drinking is the same as you would with drugs, what comes after you get the conversation off its feet can be entirely different, let alone how you keep your teen's attention. Here's what they told me has worked best.

"We need more than the facts, we need you."

I don't think parents like to hear this, but teenagers realize very clearly that ultimately our lives are in *our* hands. We all have our share of dumb decisions. Speaking only for myself, I have come to believe that most of mine come through uneducated choices. So it would seem that if I had a "dumb choice time machine," the way to correct my mistakes would be to go back and educate myself about my choices. Maybe I still would have screwed up, but at least I would have known what I was doing. By informing us about the dangers of the abuse of alcohol and cigarettes, you allow us to hear what we are not hearing from our friends and the media, and you arm us with a very powerful tool: the ability to see the whole picture, to have perspective, which can enable us to make better decisions about our lives.

Just like with drugs, we have a lot of misconceptions about smoking and drinking, and the power of knowledge can help straighten them out. Sometimes, the only way to find something out yourself is through trial and error, but the problem with trial and error is—well, the error part. Some mistakes you can laugh about later with your friends, but it's the ones that you can't that make learning about alcohol and cigarettes through self-experience a very dangerous thing.

So once again it's pretty much up to you to give us the information that will help steer us away from the whole error thing. But that is no easy task when you are dealing with us teens, who are pretty much sure that we know everything there is to know about, well . . . everything there is to know. That is why it is not just enough to blurt out facts and statistics about how drinking does this and smoking does that—there is a good chance your teenager won't believe what you throw at her. But if you can work the facts into a meaningful dialogue (there's that word again) and not just recite them like you're downloading a Web site, you'll have a better chance of getting your teen's attention. Then you can talk about what she thinks about those facts—responses that you may be surprised to hear.

Fact: Cigarettes contain nicotine, a very addictive drug. According to the American Lung Association, they also contain the following:

- Acetic acid: used in hair dye developer
- Acetone: a main ingredient in paint and fingernail polish remover
- Ammonia: a poisonous gas and powerful cleaning agent
- Arsenic: a potent poison used to kill rats
- Benzene: a poisonous toxin found in mothballs and banned from paint thinners
- Cadmium: a highly toxic chemical used in car batteries and metal plating
- Carbon monoxide: a poisonous gas that destroys red blood cells
- Formaldehyde: a foul-smelling liquid used to embalm dead bodies
- Hydrazine: used in jet and rocket fuels
- Hydrogen cyanide: a poison used in gas chambers for executions
- Nickel: used in the process of electroplating

- Pyridine: used as a chemical dog repellant spray
- Toluene: a poisonous industrial solvent banned for use in nail polish

I knew they had bad chemicals and stuff, but I didn't know about all these.

GREG, AGE 15, TUCSON, ARIZONA

Fact: According to the American Cancer Society, more Americans are killed by cigarettes than by alcohol, car accidents, suicide, AIDS, homicide, and illegal drugs combined.

Well, yeah, that makes sense, but those are only people who smoke all the time. I'm going to stop when I go to college.

FRANI, AGE 16, TALBOT, MARYLAND

Fact: According to the Centers for Disease Control and Prevention, teen smokers are 8 times more likely to use marijuana, and 22 times more likely to use cocaine.

Whatever. Smoking doesn't make kids do drugs, it's just kids who do drugs, smoke, too. I smoke and I know I won't do drugs, because I don't want to.

SALLY, AGE 17, GAINESVILLE, FLORIDA

Fact: How addictive are cigarettes? Forty percent of teenagers who smoke on a regular basis have tried to quit the habit and have been unsuccessful, according to the American Osteopathic Association.

I bet they are people who smoke a lot more than I do. I can quit whenever I want.

HARRIS, AGE 14, CORPUS CHRISTI, TX

Fact: Recent studies have also shown that teen guys who smoke heavily could experience erectile dysfunction or impotence by the time they turn 30—and this is according to an online discount cigarette supplier!

What!? That can't be true . . . I hope it's not. Wow, I never knew that.

JOEY, AGE 15, SALUDA, SOUTH CAROLINA

Fact: How hard is it to overcome a nicotine addiction? According to the U.S. Food and Drug Administration, even among adults who express a strong desire to quit smoking and who receive optimal medical care, only half of the patients studied were able to stop smoking for as long as 1 week, and the long-term failure rate was more than 80 percent after patients were withdrawn from nicotine replacement.

I didn't think nicotine was that strong. I guess that's why it's so hard for people to quit.

BOBBY, AGE 16, SAN DIEGO, CA

"It can't hurt me."

Lots of teens know about the detrimental effects of smoking and drinking but still make the decision to do both. This has to do with the "Superman Syndrome" I spoke about in the drug chapter. It makes us feel like we are invincible. For most teens, tomorrow is not in the spectrum; all that matters is today. Therefore, who cares about a couple of tequila shots and half a pack of smokes? What're they going to do to me?

It's not like I'm an alcoholic. I drink on the weekends with everybody else. I know all that stuff about my liver, but it's not like I'm totally going to kill it; that only happens if I drink like every day for 20 years.

RALPH, AGE 16, OWENSBORO, KENTUCKY

I smoke, but who cares? I took health, I know about all of the tar and shit, and how it kills those little grape things in your lungs, but I don't care. It's not like I'm going to smoke my whole life, I just like smoking with my friends, and I'll stop whenever I want to.

GRACE, AGE 13, BURBANK, CALIFORNIA

I'm not going to look down on Grace and Ralph from my high horse because I'm the same as them. I know that smoking kills your alveoli (those grape things that Grace was talking about). I know that drinking causes scar tissue to build up in your liver. I know all of it, yet I've done both on occasion. This is a conundrum—how do you help somebody who does not want to be helped? After your teens know all there is to know about their actions, the final decision is up to them, but what if they make the wrong choice?

It's clear to me that these kids really need some dialogue with their parents about the meaning behind the facts. The facts themselves aren't going to do it.

"We do what you do, not what you say."

For adults, smoking and (even more so) drinking are not only legal pastimes, they're almost expected. At almost every single adult social event you will find alcohol. At sporting events, beer is sold at the concession stand and by roaming vendors; many parents have wine at dinner or a drink or beer or two (or three) after work; and what's a cookout or picnic without a few brews or maybe some margaritas? The point is, alcohol seems to be an inextricable accent to any adult occasion. Smoking may be the same for many families, whether it's half a pack a day or just an occasional cigar. So how can you tell your kids not to drink and smoke when you have a bottle of beer in one hand and a cigarette in the other? The difference might be clear to you, but can't you see why that feels like hypocrisy to us?

> *My mom smokes about a pack a day. I don't get her—she rips my head off whenever she sees me with one in my mouth, telling me that I will kill myself, but I've probably smoked 100 packs by now just from living in the same house as her. If she can make the choice to kill herself, why can't I?*
>
> HANK, AGE 17, LAUREL, DELAWARE

> *I'm not a drinker, but I do like everyone else does—drink at parties and stuff like that. My dad is all up on me for drinking because he says that I'll like kill my liver, but he drinks all the time.*
>
> SHERI, AGE 16, ASH FORK, ARIZONA

A parent is like a cop, except it's probably more fun because you get to make up your own laws and punishments. But imagine if cops sped all the time, ran red lights, and sold crack. If they pulled you over and ticketed you for a traffic violation, you would feel violated yourself. How dare they ticket you for something that they do themselves? This is the question that many teens with parents who smoke or drink ask all the time. When these teens complain to their parents that their situation is unfair, they get responses such as, "Well, life is unfair." Or, "I am an adult and I can make my own decisions; when you are, you can, too." All true. But teens are quick to dismiss those kinds of explanations and tune out your advice.

Even if smoking and drinking are legal and accepted for you, doing so can confuse your messages to us. It's perfectly reasonable of you to say, "Hey, I'm an adult. When you're an adult, you can do these things, too." But some teens just don't buy it—especially when they see the problems these things may be causing in their parents' lives. So how can you get your teen to do what you say, not what you do? Well, to be honest, I have some bad news: The teens I talked to don't believe you can. To successfully implement laws of any kind—whether you are a police officer or a parent—you need to prove your authority and the validity of your laws by following them yourself. Teens want you to follow your words much as they have to. So I guess that leaves a question for you: How much do you want us to not drink and smoke? Enough to quit?

FROM RANTING TO PRECAUTION

So is there anything kids WILL believe and listen to? Yes, but the conversations that seemed to work best with teens may be very different than what you are used to. Teens say the most successful type of these conversations shifted gears from ranting to precaution.

"Talk to us realistically."

Teens in general tend to do the things that you, most of all, don't want them to. But the problem is that a lot of parents don't talk to their teens with this in mind. They fail to relay important information just because they don't want their teens to think that they are condoning the use of illegal substances. Teens say that conversations were the most productive when their parents took a leap of faith and realized that their teens were probably doing the things that they did not want them to. These parents were not telling their kids that drinking and smoking were okay to do, they were just taking precautions so in case the child was doing them, she wasn't hurt even worse. Basically, it comes down to giving your teen a safe way out of a potentially dangerous situation.

> *I really don't smoke, and I only drink sometimes, and not to the point where I am falling-down drunk. My mom thinks that I never drink, but she talks to me like she knows that I will. We always talk about drinking in moderation, and about drinking and driving, and other stuff.*
>
> BLAINE, AGE 16, BUFFALO, NEW YORK

Blaine's mom took that leap of faith, and like all leaps into the unknown, this one was scary. She did not want him to drink, but she knew that, as an older teen, drinking is for him more of an inevitability than a possibility. But she raised an important question: "If I talk to him about alcohol safety, will he think that I condone the use if it?" The teens that I have spoken to say that this apprehension must be overcome to have real impact and meaning during a conversation about alcohol. It seems from the interviews that I have gotten that many parents out there believe if their teens know all about the dangers of drinking and smoking, they will make the decision not to do either. Facts about scar tissue buildup are nice but will deter only some teens from drinking, and trust me that "some" is by far the minority of the group. The leap of faith is to accept that we will most likely drink in the future or may be drinking now, and since you will probably never know about it, it's better not to take the risk, so prepare us realistically, not idealistically. Claudia's mom took that leap because of a personal situation.

"Give us rules to remember that can protect us."

I'm not a bad kid, but I do drink occasionally at parties and stuff, but it's really not a big deal, everyone does it. My mom has this rule with me; she calls it the "drink down rule." If I have a drink and I put it down I cannot pick it up. She has this rule because she had a few friends of hers that were raped because people put roofies and stuff in their drinks when they put them down at a party. I know my mom doesn' t want me to drink, but I think it' s cool that she speaks to me like I am an adult, and she realizes that I will.

CLAUDIA, AGE 16, PORT ARTHUR, TEXAS

Even though 16 is not even close to being an adult, Claudia and millions of other teens in the United States find themselves in situations where they will need to be making adult decisions. Claudia's mom obviously does not allow her 16-year-old to drink, but she put safety in front of idealism, making sure that on the chance that her daughter would drink, she would have the knowledge to keep herself safe. I understand that this is hard to do. You may feel, in a way, that you are saying to your teens that it is okay if you drink, just do it in the right way. But the many teens that I talked to who had parents that talked to them about alcohol *safety* said that they felt like they were speaking on a different level because they were being talked to more as a peer than a child, something that we all want to feel. This different level is one where you feel you can speak to us frankly, without having to walk on the eggshells of adolescence, which can cause you to filter out certain crucial information that we may need in the future.

THE BIG FEARS

Even if you're one of the parents who thinks maybe it's okay—or just inevitable—that your teenager occasionally has a drink or a smoke, I'm sure you still live in fear that your child or his friends may be drinking and driving, binge drinking, or developing a drinking problem. Here's how some parents have been effective in addressing these issues with their kids.

Drinking and Driving

Alcohol can be a very fun thing, but when mixed with a ton of moving steel, it can become deadly. According to the National Highway Traffic Safety Administration, in the year 2000 there were 2,339 youths killed in alcohol-related crashes, which was 36.6 percent of total youth traffic fatalities. For some reason, despite knowing all the dangers of drinking and driving, too many teenagers still do it.

Why? I spoke to Barry, who was one of the luckier teens who was caught drinking and driving by the police, not The Reaper.

I was at this beach party down by South Beach, it was off the hook, and there were hot girls and drinking everywhere. It must have been like 4:00 in the morning, and things were still going strong, but I had work the next morning at 9:00, so I just got in my car and left. I didn't think that I was that drunk when I was walking to my car, but when I started driving I could tell that I was a little off. I must have been swerving around or something because like 5 minutes later I saw those lights behind me. I got slapped with a huge fine and got my license taken away. That night sucked.

BARRY, AGE 17, MIAMI, FLORIDA

My mother and other parents have told me time and time again that one of their biggest fears, once their teens get their licenses, is that they will drive drunk. My mom has this speech that she always gives me when I go out with my friends; I have heard it so many times I can repeat it verbatim. It goes like this: "If you have anything to drink—I mean *anything*—you do not get into a car! Do you hear me, *do* you hear me!?" followed by a quick, "Yes, Mom" by me, and then a "Do you promise?" and another "Yes, Mom." I have spoken to many teens who can also repeat their mom's or dad's drunk-driving speech to a T, yet a bunch of them have admitted to at least driving tipsy at one time or another.

The question many parents have is, why would Barry drive? Well, he claimed that he didn't think that he was *that* drunk, but how drunk is that drunk? What number of drinks allows you to put your and other people's lives in danger? This is a question that many teens do not ask themselves. Since your last-minute reminders are not cutting it, what else can you do? How can you help us make the right decision and not get into a car drunk and end up like Danielle?

I was with about six friends of mine and we all went to this party for graduation from junior year. We were all smashed, and so was everyone else at the party. I was only going to have like two drinks early in the night because I had a fight with my dad the night before and he was making me come back early. Well, I had like two shots, then I funneled a few beers, and it put me over the edge. I was so afraid of being screamed at by my dad if I did not come home at 11:00 that I decided to drive. I didn't even make it down the kid's driveway. I ran over their mailbox and into a parked car. I was fine, but the cars weren't.

DANIELLE, AGE 15, ROCHESTER, NEW YORK

I spoke to some teens about Danielle's story, and a few of them told about a deal they have with their parents that keeps them from driving drunk and ending up with a Danielle story of their own. When I asked them why they or any of their friends have driven drunk, the most common response was that there was no way around it, they had to. Well, the plan that these teens' parents worked out for them solves this problem: It gives them an outlet so there *is* a way out. The way it works is that if they are sober at a party where there is drinking and no one can give them a ride home because they all are drunk, their parents will come and pick them up.

But not only will they pick them up: They won't get yelled at for being at a party where people were drinking. When I told some parents this, they thought that it was a great idea, and they were more than willing to implement the same program with their kids. But then I told them about a more common and realistic variation of this situation—one that other teens and I feel is more important. In this variation not only has your teen gotten himself in a situation where no one can drive him home because they're drunk, *he* is, too. Even if this was the case, he could call his parents and they would pick him up from wherever he was. Still, for most of the teens that I talked with whose parents implemented this plan, the deal was that they wouldn't get yelled at because they were taking responsibility for themselves and not getting into a car drunk.

When I spoke to my mom and some of her friends about this one, they were a lot more apprehensive. Most thought that it was kind of ridiculous for the parents to agree not to yell at their kid, because even though they did the right thing by not drinking and driving they did the wrong (not to mention illegal) thing by drinking in the first place. It's like commending your kid for stealing a gun but having the willpower not to shoot anyone. And on top of that, they felt like they would be turned from parents into some sort of drunk's limo service. I understood 100 percent where they were coming from, and when I told their views to teens, they also felt that it was a little implausible not to get in trouble at all. But some of the teens I talked with would rather take the chance of driving than face the wrath of their parents. Well, I also talked to a few teens who worked out a slightly different plan with their parents that seemed to be a happy medium between the first and second scenario.

> *My mom and dad have this thing with me to keep me from driving drunk. What happens is, if I can't drive or no one else can drive, I can give them a call and they will pick me up. They will not yell at me that night (usually they won't say anything at all), but the next morning, we'll have a conversation. Part of the deal is that since they didn't yell at me, I have to talk with them the next morning. But it's not like I can just get drunk whenever I want and then call my dad to come pick me up; they have to be absolute emergencies.*
>
> LANDA, 17, AMHERST, MASSACHUSETTS

What Landa's parents did was devise a system that was both reasonable and safe. Landa does not have to be apprehensive about calling her parents because she knows that she won't get yelled at, but she also knows that she inconvenienced them and now owes them a conversation, whether she likes it or not. This conversation is a very important one. Think of it as a power play in hockey: Your teen screwed up and now he or she has a team member in the penalty box. You'll have a limited time period to score, or in this case *reach* a goal, but you'll have a much easier time doing it because, unlike in most conversations you have with your teen about drinking, you have the upper hand. Your teen owes you this one. Just because this conversation is one that you are entitled to doesn't mean that you are guaranteed to have a productive one. Teens have told me that you still need to remember the basic conversation rules so that you can facilitate open speech. Things like not lecturing, and remembering to keep things third person as much as possible, will ensure that your little chat will truly be a powerful one, and one that your teenager will remember.

Binge Drinking

Drinking in moderation and in proportion is not a dangerous thing if done responsibly, but where teen drinking is concerned, moderation, proportion, and responsibility usually do not enter the picture. While you may be totally content sipping on a glass of wine or nursing a beer all night, most teens would not. For most of us teens, when we drink, we drink for no other reason than the effect: We drink to get drunk. Because of this, binge-drinking is one of the most common ways that teens today drink. Obviously, what many teens do not realize is that this behavior can come with dangerous ramifications.

> *I was out partying with my friends in the city. We were hopping from bar to bar and I guess you could say I'm an attractive girl. There was no shortage of people offering to buy me drinks and I was not about to say no. I don't even know how many shots of vodka I took, but I took them all so fast that the last thing that I felt was tipsy. The next thing I remember was waking up in the hospital after getting my stomach pumped.*
>
> KAYLEEN, AGE 18, QUEENS, NEW YORK

According to The National Clearinghouse for Alcohol and Drug Information, "When excessive amounts of alcohol are consumed, the brain is deprived of oxygen. The struggle to deal with an overdose of alcohol and lack of oxygen will eventually cause the brain to shut down the voluntary functions that regulate breathing and heart rate." In laymen's terms, having severe alcohol poisoning without seeking medical help means you die. End of story. And that is the real danger of binge drinking: You have so many drinks in succession that by the time you realize you're drunk and should stop drinking, it's too late. You've already had too many drinks for your system to handle.

I remember visiting my sister in college and seeing an ambulance almost every night on campus because some teen drank too much. It is not like these people wanted this to happen; they just didn't realize the effect alcohol could have on them.

> ***My brother was having a party at our house when my mom and dad were gone. This girl Stacy came over, already drunk. I don't know how drunk she was but she passed out and turned a blue color. My brother was so scared that he would get in trouble if he called the police, so he tried to handle it himself. We tried to wake her up for a long time but couldn't. Finally my brother called a friend of his who could drive, and he came over and took her to the hospital. But she didn't make it.***
>
> **CONNER, AGE 14, GORMAN, CALIFORNIA**

Conner's brother's lack of knowledge combined with his fear of legal ramifications cost Stacy her life. It is important when talking with your teens about how to handle situations like this one that you explain the importance of *never* taking a chance with someone's life, because there is no amount of trouble worth playing with death. Conner's story was a real eye-opener to me, but the thing that scared me the most about his story was the reaction I got from teens when I asked them what *they* would do in a similar situation. Most of them had the wrong answers, and in situations like these, there is no margin for error.

When it came to talking about binge drinking, teens say that it takes the same leap of faith as talking to us about drinking and driving. Without stepping over the threshold of thinking that you are condoning your teen's drinking, you'll never be able to talk about things that could make a real difference.

This conversation tactic might seem focused toward a more advanced teen audience, but, from what I can deduce from the younger teens I spoke with, they may be doing things well beyond what you think they are capable of. Plus, of the teens I talked to whose parents informed them of the truth about drinking (and smoking, for that matter) and who subsequently decided not to drink or smoke, almost all were talked to at a young age, (about 10 to 13 years). The truth of the matter is, we teens grow up pretty fast these days, and the longer you wait to have these types of conversations, the longer your teen is denied information that could save her—or someone else's—life.

My mom and dad talked with me all about alcohol poisoning when I was a kid. I was kind of a dork and I never went to parties during my teen years, so I never had the chance to put what they told me to use—until I went to college. I went to a school in Washington, D.C., and in the first 3 years I was there I had to call an ambulance four times because someone had alcohol poisoning. Every time except one happened the same way: I get off work late, show up at a party where everyone is drunk, some freshman girl is on the couch that everyone thinks is just passed out, I find out she has alcohol poisoning, and I call an ambulance. All of those girls could have died if I was not there. It's not like I was the only one sober enough to think, I was just the only one who knew better, and knew that those girls were not just "passed out."

MOHAMMED, AGE 24, TOWNSEND, DELAWARE

Problem Drinking

Talking to your teens about binge drinking is very important, but what do you do if you think that your teen himself has a drinking problem? Teens say the first thing you should do is compare your suspicions to the actual signs of someone with a drinking problem so that you don't peg your teen as something she is not. There are many good Web sites where you can find this information. (See "Resources" on page 269.)

My mom had this Fourth of July party. Everyone was drinking, so no one really cared that I did. I had a great time being tipsy like everyone else. The next day my mom came into my room, sat on the end of my bed, and said, "Ben, are you going to admit you have a problem?" I had no clue what she was talking about. She went on to tell me that I had a drinking problem and that I needed to admit it. When I asked her why she thought this, she said that whenever I drink I get drunk. Then I asked her when she saw this, and the only one she could come up with was the night before. All I could do was laugh.

Ben, age 18, Ramona, Kansas

Unjustifiedly accusing your teen of a drinking problem will do nothing other than alienate her. If you confront your teen without tangible examples of her actions, she will have a much easier time brushing off your accusations. But teens have told me that confrontation should not be your first step. If you suspect that your teen may have a drinking problem, opening up lines of communication so that she has a chance to talk with you about it should be your first step. If that isn't working, then I guess you have to find a way to confront your teen in a positive way. I can't say that teenagers welcome this strategy, but if you've tried other, gentler methods and they're not working, I'm sure you're going to want to do it.

When you do, think about this. Teens have told me that you will have a better chance at having a successful confrontation when you come from a place of concern, understanding, and acceptance, and not of accusation, anger, or betrayal. These feelings might be hard for you to curb, but teenagers pick up on them fast and can shut down if it feels like we are getting a scolding instead of a conversation.

One method that worked for many teens I talked to was when their parents asked about their friends' friends. After they started up a conversation about alcohol abuse, they asked their teens if they knew anyone who they thought might have a drinking problem. This way your teen can vicariously talk about any drinking problems he might be having, without feeling that he is giving away any information about himself or his close friends. Then you can continue to talk with your teen about these "other kids" and together try to understand why "they" are drinking and how to get "them" help.

This method is most effective with teens who realize they may have a problem (something that studies show very few do). So part of the talk may also be about what constitutes a drinking problem so they can see themselves in the verbal mirror you're holding up to them.

Cracking the Code:

A Mom's View on What a Parent Can Do

This is about the scariest chapter here because Rhett seems to be passing on the message that there's not much chance of getting through to your kids *at all* on the dangers of cigarettes and alcohol, and we know that in terms of the actual chance of something awful happening to your kids, there's probably nothing more scary than alcohol.

Rhett puts cigarettes and alcohol together because teens think of them together: the stuff that's not really drugs, so there's no big deal about doing them.

"I wouldn't lump cigarettes in with alcohol," Dr. Joseph Yampolsky, a licensed psychologist, told me. Kids use cigarettes and alcohol for different reasons, he pointed out, and they're drawn to them for different reasons.

"Teenagers use alcohol for just two reasons," Dr. Yampolsky says. "In that, they're different from adults, and they don't know this. They say, 'Mom and Dad do it,' but where much of adult drinking is done in a social context, a social milieu, teens drink to get drunk, or as a form of self-medication."

That certainly fits in with what Rhett says. "While you may be totally content sipping on a glass of wine or nursing a beer all night, most teens would not . . . we drink to get drunk." That makes me shudder, too. I wonder if it's one of those areas where teens do understand the difference but think that they're right, and adults just don't get it.

I also wonder if kids know that they're being crazy, even if they won't admit it to us, because at the same time that they're saying, "You parents may drink in moderation, but that's not for us gutsy teens," they're also saying, "We don't really drink that much."

According to a study by Dan Segrist, Ph.D., professor of psychology at Southwestern Illinois College, *teenagers, in general, think that they drink less than their friends do.* In fact, Segrist discovered, the average teenage boy thinks that his friends drink twice as much as he does: A teenager who binge-drinks twice a month will generally assume that his friends binge-drink four times a month.

This is based on nothing but perception—nothing but wishful thinking. "I don't really have a drinking problem—heck, everyone else drinks more than I do. Sure, I had four or five drinks at the party, but that was nothing. All the other guys were having seven or eight drinks."

This may be dicey information to try to use when you take on a skilled teenage debater. "Everyone else drinks more than I do? See, that proves I'm okay. Everyone else doesn't drink more than I do? See, that proves teenagers are all right; it's not really a problem."

But any time anyone tries to take both sides of an issue, that means there's some guilt there, and exploiting guilt should be what we do best. Communication is the key here, as it is everywhere. Don't assume you aren't getting through. We always get through more than kids like to let on that we do.

In addition, Dr. Yampolsky counsels, setting a good example is crucial. "You have to be realistic. Society does view alcohol as okay. But you can set a tone with your own behavior."

"**Don't** hide the fact that you drink—your kid will find out."

"**Do** set a good example. Drink responsibly; carry yourself responsibly. You are your kids' best role model."

"**Do** keep talking, keep communicating. Set limits. Be rational—be aware that kids won't always stay within those limits, but set realistic consequences for breaking them."

I set up the Amnesty Rule with my kids. If you're in a situation where drinking has caused problems—you've gotten drunk, you're at a party where things are starting to happen that you don't like, your ride has been drinking—wherever you are, whatever time it is, you can call and I'll come get you. And you'll have amnesty . . . for 24 hours. For 24 hours I won't question you, I won't lecture you, I won't punish you. After that, yes, there'll be appropriate consequences. Behavior always has consequences. But the first thing is to get you out of the situation, with no judgment and no questions.

And here's something about communication, and how kids hear more than they let on, that I found out by accident. My daughter Kyle told me she had been at parties where kids just chugged down shots to get as drunk as possible as fast as possible, and throw up all over their shoes (or their dates). She hated it, she told me, but she didn't know how to finesse her way out of the situation.

"Why don't you say that you're taking antihistamines for an allergy, and you can't drink?" I suggested.

She gave me the classic Withering Teenage Look. "That is the dumbest, dorkiest idea I ever heard," she said. "I would never use a line like that."

End of conversation. Fast-forward about 4 or 5 months. I wandered into the kitchen while Kyle was on the phone with a friend. "I guess I'll pass on the party," I heard her saying. "I'm taking antihistamines for an allergy, and I'm not allowed to drink anything at all."

If your teen is drinking to self-medicate, this is a really serious business, and it requires intervention, counseling, and whatever it takes. Dr. Yampolsky points out that there's a striking connection between this form of drinking and learning disabilities, and that all too often, parents don't realize this. We buy into the Spring Break image: teenage party animals. We forget that even among teens, there are solitary drinkers, seeking refuge from a world they can't handle.

Smoking, says Dr. Yampolsky, is a completely different situation. Kids drink to get high, or to self-medicate, but they smoke to look cool.

"Teenage smoking stems from the need for affiliation. This is one of the strongest needs teenagers have, and they don't always recognize it. Rhett's interviews show that. None of his respondents said anything about the need to belong, or to be like their friends."

(Chances are, your kids aren't going to believe the research on this. I mentioned Dr. Yampolsky's findings to Rhett, and he said, "That's dumb. None of my friends or I have any need for affiliation when it comes to smoking." I guess it's not cool to try to be cool.)

You probably can't stop your kids from smoking. And you can't stop your kids from feeling peer pressure, either. But you can point out the connection, and you can discuss peer pressure issues in general. That should be one of the ongoing conversations you have with your kids, and not just on the level of "If your friends jumped off a bridge, would you jump, too?"

What works for smoking? Dr. Yampolsky is emphatic on one point: Scare tactics do *not*. You can't tell your kids about what might happen to them in 30 years and expect it to make any difference at all. Your best bet is to try to find ways ("Do you really like those yellow stains on your teeth?") to make it seem uncool *now.*

Is it hopeless? Are all kids going to drink and smoke, no matter what you do? Rhett's statistics make it sound that way. But I started thinking, and it occurred to me: I'd be included in those statistics, that seven out of ten who've tried smoking cigarettes, and eight out of ten who've tried alcohol.

I tried smoking when I was a teenager . . . once. Got sick, decided it wasn't for me. I have friends who had the same experience with drinking. Tried it once, and never again. But we'd be counted in that statistic.

The same survey from the Centers for Disease Control and Prevention from which Rhett got his eight-out-of-ten statistic also said that:

- About 52 percent of students had at least one drink of alcohol during the 30 days preceding the survey
- Nearly 33 percent of students had five or more drinks of alcohol on at least one occasion during the 30 days preceding the survey (i.e., engaged in episodic heavy drinking)

These are scary—and sobering—statistics. But it's not eight out of ten. Not all teens are drinking, not all teens are binge-drinking. You do have a chance to get through to your kids. Don't stop trying.

Chapter 3

SEX

I remember the first time I talked to my mom about sex. I was about 6 years old at the time (so I have some excuse for this story). My mom had taken my sister and me to a huge, crowded movie theater in Manhattan, where we were living at the time. We went to see *Father of the Bride* with Steve Martin. It was mostly a nice movie to take kids to, but there was this one part where Steve Martin, the father, has just figured out that his little "innocent" daughter, who is 23, is having sex with her fiancé. Steve Martin gets all flustered and embarrassed when the couple is about to go for a ride in the car, and blurts out, "Don't forget to fasten your condoms!"

The audience laughed, all 1,000 of them. Then, when it

quieted down, I turned to my mother and said, in a booming 6-year-old voice, "Are they going to have sex?" Everyone in the whole place turned and looked at us to hear what my mother was going to say to me. She just said, "Uh huh, yes, honey."

Ignoring a smattering of muffled laughs, I said with great concern, "Mom, I thought you told me you die when you have sex!" Now 1,000 people were laughing even harder than they had at Steve Martin, and my mom decided the simplest thing to do, under the circumstances, was just to repeat, "Uh huh, yes, that's right, honey."

Now, before you think my mom was a crazy woman trying to scare the crap out of a poor little kid, it turned out she hadn't actually told me that, exactly. I had overheard a conversation that my mom had with my older sister about AIDS, how you can get it, and what can happen to you when you have it. So I just connected the dots incorrectly. But that didn't make my mom feel any less embarrassed.

Before you write off my experience at the movies as just a cute story about a 6-year-old child, there may be some lessons here for us. First, if you don't discuss things carefully with kids, they (even older kids) may well take partial information and jump to bizarre conclusions. And kids don't stay 6 years old forever. They grow up and are forced into situations where they will have to make decisions on their own, and these days that happens at younger and younger ages. So while it's cute at 6, if your kids are still spouting misinformation—and maybe even acting on it—in later years, things stop being cute and start getting scary.

You have to find ways to say the things you need to and still get through the embarrassment of the situation—as well as overcome the dreaded "teen wall" that some of us put up to keep parents from being too nosy. This is a lot easier said than done, but with the help of hundreds of teens across the United States, this "teen wall" needn't be so impenetrable.

Here's what they told me that parents should know about talking to us about sex. Even though some of it may be difficult to listen to, I hope it helps you understand where we're coming from and helps you communicate with us better.

STUFF YOU MAY NOT WANT TO HEAR

There's a lot in this book that is encouraging for parents to hear—but then again, there's stuff you may find just plain scary. Sex is one of those areas with a high Scary Quotient, so brace yourself. Here is what a lot of kids told me about the role of sex in their lives.

"My friends told me everything I need to know."

When I surveyed teenagers about sex, all too many of them gave responses like this when I asked if they'd gotten anything out of sex conversations with their parents.

> *I didn't even listen because I already know everything about sex from my friends, so why do I have to hear it from my parents? What do my parents know? Everything's different from when they were young. They didn't even do half the things we do now.*
>
> SHELLY, AGE 14, ENCINO, CALIFORNIA

By the time you get around to giving The Talk, it may be harder than you think. If you don't start talking to your kids early, it's not going to take any time at all before they think they know more than you. Then, don't count on them listening.

The worst part of it is that when you talk to these kids who "know" all about sex from their friends, there is a good chance that they know a lot of stuff that's wrong, and that could potentially get them in trouble. I asked 14-year-old Shelly if she had protected sex, and she said no. When I asked her why not, she said, "I'm too young to get pregnant. You can't get pregnant until you're a junior in high school."

How about all those 12-year-old girls—and younger—on maternity wards? But her friends had told her she was safe until she was a junior, and even I wasn't able to convince her otherwise.

So I started asking around about what other kids who "knew" everything about sex *really* knew. And here are a few things I heard.

- "I won't get AIDS. Only gay people get that."
- "You can't get pregnant if you have sex during your period."
- "You can't get a girl pregnant if you pull out just as you feel yourself starting to get all hot."
- "You can't get pregnant if you wash yourself out a lot after intercourse."
- "You can't get a girl pregnant if you have more than .05 blood alcohol content because it kills the sperm, so all you have to do is get drunk enough and you're safe."

So, as much as we teenagers think we know about sex, many of us are dead wrong. Along with straightening out the myths and misinformation they may have picked up from their friends, talking about the dangers and the responsibilities that go along with sex is the *most* crucial thing a parent can do. But before you can talk to us you need to know how we feel and think about sex. It may be quite different than you expect.

"Oral sex is not sex."

Of all of the teens that I interviewed on this topic, it seemed like maybe one or two in a hundred considered oral sex to be sex. I'm guessing a lot of parents don't agree. I don't know if you're going to be able to change that perception, but you should realize that's probably how your teen—and probably even your preteen—thinks.

When I was in seventh grade, to have oral sex was a big deal: We only knew one kid in the whole grade who said he did it (but most of us thought he was lying). By mid-year eighth grade, oral sex was no big deal—everyone said they were doing it (and this time we knew they weren't lying). By the time high school rolled around, giving and receiving oral sex became so normal that it was basically expected, even in casual hook-ups.

So even if your teen is listening to you or his health teacher talking about the dangers of "sex" and believes you, you may not be out of the woods. If we don't think oral sex *is* sex, then it can't be dangerous, right? It's clear that teenagers need a separate conversation about this so we realize the dangers of oral sex may be different from—but just as real as—the ones we associate with "real sex."

"Scaring me isn't going to work for very long."

Parents try their hardest to keep their kids from making unwise decisions, and unfortunately the way things go with a teen, that is a hard task to achieve. I have found that to do this many parents resort to using scare tactics. The great thing about scare tactics is that they really work—for a while. You can bet I was not even going to think about having sex when I was 6, knowing I was going to die. But the effect of scare tactics eventually wears off. When we are young and impressionable, your word is our creed; when we hear some horrific thing about sex and its consequences, you can be sure we'll take it not only to heart but to the playground, where all of our friends will find out about our newly acquired information. Eventually we go from living through your words and experiences to living our own, and this is when we find out that Mommy and Daddy may not have been telling us the whole truth and nothing but the truth.

When I was about 7, I touched a hot pan and burned myself. My mom told me that is what vaginas do.

Rick, age 14, Salem, Ohio

Well, this one certainly brings new meaning to the saying, "She's hot."

Ouch! But how is a 7-year-old supposed to know his mother is lying to him? This means Rick lived for years thinking that using protection while having sex meant bringing a fire extinguisher. When Rick got older and eventually found out that what his mother told him was not true, the only thing that got burnt was his mom's ability to continue to talk with him about sex. How is he supposed to trust anything his mother says about sex if she has already proven that she is willing to lie to him?

> *My mom only ever gave me one piece of advice about sex, and it was pretty weird. When I had my first period, no one had ever told me anything about it, and I didn't know what it meant. So I asked my mom, and she said, "You're going to have this every month for the rest of your life, and you can never ever let a man touch you there." That was it. So I asked around in school the next day, and I found out about it, and from then on, if I needed to know anything, I asked my friends. I knew I wasn't going to get anything from my mom.*
>
> MARY BETH, AGE 16, AMSTERDAM, NEW YORK

Lying to your kids about sex might quell their curiosity for now, but it will soon come back and bite your communication in the butt.

"If you're just being nosy, I'm not talking."

Using a sex discussion to try to pry into your child's personal life is a fail-safe way to ruin a conversation. When you ask us any personal information about ourselves during a sex conversation, it puts us in a terribly uncomfortable position, and for many kids that's an instant off switch.

My dad took me into his home office when I was like 14 and told me to sit down. He said it was time that he told me about the facts of life. So he's like, this and that, and I'm like, "Sure, Dad, sure, I know all that," and suddenly he's really pissed off, and he's yelling at me, "How come you know so much about this? What have you been doing? Are you having sex?" That was the last time I ever talked to my dad about that stuff. How could he expect me to talk with him if he is forcing me to tell him things I would never want him to know?

LEAH, AGE 17, BELLINGHAM, WASHINGTON

I asked what was so bad about parents asking teens about their sex lives.

I would never ask them about their sex lives! That stuff is personal. I expect them to respect my privacy just like I respect theirs.

JACK, AGE 18, QUEENS, NEW YORK

Why do they want to know? The only reason they'd have is so they can use it against you. Sure, Sid, we just want to know so we can understand you better. Right. I'm not stupid—I know if I say, "Yeah, I've had sex," I'll never be allowed to get within 50 yards of a boy.

SID, AGE 16, MORRISTOWN, NEW JERSEY

The way I see it, knowing if your teen has gone to first, second, or third base doesn't matter. The conversations you're having with us should be had at any level of sexual maturity. You'll probably never know exactly what your teenager has done sexually, so you're probably better off assuming that they've done a lot more than you think they have. *Note:* Almost all of the teens I talked with said they were more sexually experienced than their parents thought they were. Asking your teen about her sex life will get you nowhere, especially if you haven't built up trust with her in talking about sex. When pushed too hard to kiss and tell, we'll most likely just lie to you, and on top of that you'll shut yourself off as a person that we feel we can trust and talk to freely and comfortably.

MAKING DIFFICULT CONVERSATIONS A LITTLE EASIER

I can't imagine a sex talk ever being easy, but it doesn't have to be as difficult and problematic as most teens make it out to be. In fact, a few parents have found some pretty good ways to have meaningful talks with their children with a minimum amount of embarrassment and a maximum amount of helpful advice.

Here is some of what's worked best for teens.

"Talk to me in a place where I feel comfortable, at a time I feel comfortable."

When talking to your kids about a subject as uncomfortable as sex, little things can cause big problems. Many teens have told me that staging your conversations at the right time and in the right place can help keep the level of discomfort down, meaning you're keeping productivity up. There were a lot of differences in when and where kids preferred to talk, so what it really came down to was figuring out which would work best for your teen. But just to narrow down the field, here is what some teens said worked and didn't work for them.

I liked it that when my mom talked to me about sex issues she did it in the car, on the way to band practice. I didn't have to look at her in the eyes because she was driving, and I knew that it couldn't last that long because practice is only 10 minutes away.

KELLY, AGE 14, BOONTON, NEW JERSEY

Knowing there is a time limit to a sex conversation—one within sight—helps us not feel like we are indefinitely trapped in a talk. But using the car too much can backfire. For some parents, because of their work schedules, the only time they can really talk privately to their kids is in the car. But too much of a good thing can be bad. For one, it brings formality to your conversations, something you definitely want to avoid. If every time you pick up your teen you talk about sex, she'll feel like she has a dreaded appointment with you. (And of course, we don't want you to steer over the curb when we ask you whether you think oral sex is really sex.) Uncomfortable conversations, like those about sex, work better when they seem unplanned and unexpected. The more casual and normal they seem to you, the more casual and normal they will seem to us.

There are other ways to have a finite conversation than just in the car. Other times that teens said worked well was starting conversations right before bedtime, or before the school bus comes, or before a favorite TV show. When we feel trapped, just like anyone feeling trapped, all we can think about is how we can get out of our situation. When we can see the end of a sex conversation at the beginning, there is a better chance that we will pay attention to you, and not just be on the lookout for an escape route.

Many other teens gave me examples of where they would feel the most comfortable talking to you. Again, it's a question that you'll have to answer with your own teenager—there was some difference in opinion on exactly where it should be. But almost every teen had a preference.

Many of them wanted the talk in their room—on their turf. They didn't want to be separated from their normal environment to have a sex conversation. Many teens have told me that their parents have the tendency of moving them into a certain room where they have all of their "important conversations," sex included. When you bring us into one of these "designated areas," it makes us feel like you have the upper hand because we are in *your* territory. I know if my mom calls me into the living room something is wrong, and immediately I feel uncomfortable. Now if she brought me in there to have a sex conversation . . . forget about it, that's full-fledged distress. On the other hand, some teens thought that coming into their room was an invasion of privacy.

Many teens said talking in common meeting areas like the kitchen or family room works best. There, not only did they feel like they were on an equal footing for conversation, they also felt like this kept the conversations more laid-back and normal, two things that should have a positive effect.

> *When my dad talks to me about sex we're normally in the kitchen just talking. I don't really mind it; it doesn't make me feel weird or anything. But I hate when he comes into my room and does it. I feel like I'm in trouble or something.*
>
> MARK, AGE 13, CHATTANOOGA, TENNESSEE

"I would rather have my mom talk to me about sex."

Another thing to consider before having a sex conversation with your teen is which parent should have it.

> *For some reason it just makes me feel weird when my dad talks to me about sex.*
>
> MARYANNE, AGE 13, STANLEY, NEW MEXICO

Sex is a unique conversation because there are differences between your talks with a boy and your talks with a girl. Because of this, some teens say that they would rather have the same-sex parent talk to them. Of course this can differ from teen to teen, so it's up to you to gauge which one of you your teen feels more comfortable talking with. But I stress *which*

ONE. Many teens have told me that sex conversations go more smoothly for them when only one parent talks to them at a time. Sometimes, when parents talk to us about sex in tandem, we feel like we are being ganged up on, and spoken *at,* not with. Staying solo will keep us from feeling overwhelmed by formality and pure numbers.

"Take the time to answer all my questions. Then I know I can keep asking you stuff."

Once in a while, mostly when we are younger, we will come to you and ask a question having to do with sex. These situations are few and far between, but the way you handle each of them can have a lasting effect. I cannot stress enough the importance of answering every question we ask, seriously and honestly. Here's a story I actually got from a father, which illustrates the importance of this point.

> *When my daughter was in sixth grade, she came home one day and asked me what a dildo was. It really took me by surprise, and I didn't know what to say, except "Let's not talk about that now. You're too young." So the next day she came home from school and said, "I asked around, and now I know what a dildo is." From that day on, I knew exactly what she was thinking: I don't need you to tell me about sex. I can find out on my own.*
>
> STEPHEN, AGE 45, POUGHKEEPSIE, NEW YORK

Stephen is exactly right. Unfortunately, sometimes when it comes to these matters you have one chance at bat. Either you hit a home run, or you are out for the season—there is no in-between.

When I was a little kid, maybe 10 years old, I asked my dad what a blow job meant. He told me, sort of, but it was in this semi-annoyed and angry voice, and it just made me feel so bad about asking that to this day I don't really talk to my dad about sex issues.

JIM, AGE 18, BANGOR, MAINE

One thing I can tell you for sure. However hard it is for you to talk to your kids about sex, it's 100 times harder for us to talk to you, especially as our bodies and feelings start changing. It takes a lot of courage to come and ask you questions; we are putting ourselves out on the line and testing the waters to see if you are someone we can go to. We really do want you to be there for us right from the start, but if we think you're not going to be honest or you're going to be mad at us, we'll find answers somewhere else. So it's a matter of asking yourself: Who do I want explaining this stuff to my teen, me or some kid at school who's been sneaking into his parent's porn collection?

"When my dad uses 'that' word, I can't listen to him anymore."

The teens I have spoken to say sex in particular is sometimes difficult to talk about with their parents. This is because they are speaking to their kids about things the kids know they've done or experienced. Picturing your dad smoking a joint is not something that is going to scar you for life, but picturing him, well, . . . you get the idea. Because of this, little things that you can do to keep these thoughts out of our heads will keep us listening.

One way is the choice of words. Some teens have told me that using words like "penis" and "vagina" can cause them to turn off during a sex conversation. This might sound silly and immature, and maybe it is. But really, I don't think those are words you use every day with your parents, either, are they? My point is not whether teens are mature, but that avoiding certain words can help us listen.

I asked a bunch of teens in an online chat about what they feel about the "hot button" words parents use, and here's what I got.

They kinda weird me out. It's so funny when my dad tries to talk to me about sex. He looks so weird right before he's about to say something like "vagina." He stutters and then his voice gets low like he is about to give a speech.

TARA, AGE 13, ERIE, PENNSYLVANIA

I have to pinch myself hard in the leg to keep from laughing when I hear my mom say "penis." I don't know, it's not like I can't hear sex words, it's just when they come out of my parents' mouths, they seem 100 times worse.

BOB, AGE 15, ST. CLOUD, MINNESOTA

I don't think there's anything wrong with it. My parents used those words all the time when I was growing up, so I'm used to them.

HELAINE, AGE 15, SCOTTSDALE, ARIZONA

I know you're thinking, "Then how can I talk about sex if I can't use the words to speak about it?" I asked teens what words they'd rather hear their parents say, and for the most part they didn't have any ideas, except "not those." The best advice I heard was that when you are talking to your teenager about sex and you see that she is cringing at certain words you say, ask her what words you should use that will make her *not* feel so uncomfortable. She may not have any better ideas, but at least you've given her the chance to comment on it.

The truth is, this will not be that big an issue. Conversations about where babies come from and what all the parts of the body are called should happen long before we're teenagers (if they haven't, I think you have bigger things to worry about). By now, the bulk of the sex conversations have more to do with knowing the responsibilities that go along with it, not naming human anatomy.

"If I tell you I'm having sex, please listen. Don't just freak out."

What if your child *does* tell you that she has had sex? If we do this, we're looking for a reaction. Teens opening up to their parents and telling them personal information is rare, but we do it for a reason. Either we really want to ask you questions, or it's probably some kind of test to see how you handle it. If you have an angry reaction—or just signal in some way that you do not want to know—it sends a bad message. This is your chance to have a great conversation. Because we were the ones who came to you, we obviously want to talk, and we will. The more you listen and show interest, the more we will feel like you really care, and the more open we will be.

The best response I've heard to a confession like this was when the parent said something like, "Well, how did you feel about it?" rather than freaking out and angrily demanding to know details about with whom and where and when. When you ask how they felt about it, a few things can occur. They might tell you that they loved it, that they hated it, they could tell you their problems pertaining to it, or they could say nothing at all because they just don't know what to say. If you sense there's something more that they want to tell you but haven't, especially if they just say "Sure, I liked it," in a hesitant type of way, then it's okay to say, "Well, a lot of the time people do not like it for various reasons," and then talk about some of the reasons. By doing that, you have opened up the gates for us to tell you what we *really* feel. It is important to tell us that having problems about sex is a very normal thing, and if we have any sort of problems down the line, we can always come to you. This doesn't at all guarantee that we will, but depending how this conversation goes, there is a good chance that we might bring it up again down the line.

One more thing to remember is not to push too far and probe too much all at once. If it gets to a point in the conversation where your teen seems very uncomfortable, it's time for you to butt out gracefully. Try another time, and perhaps a different method, to bring up the subject again.

THE STUFF THAT'S EVEN HARDER TO TALK ABOUT

News flash: Teenagers are going to make mistakes. But when it comes to sex, some are much bigger than others. And no matter what we do, we want our parents to be on our side. But a lot of teens worry whether that's really going to be the case if something happens.

"I'm afraid of what you'll say if I get pregnant."

We teens have to handle a lot of responsibility in our lives. Most we can handle ourselves, but there are a few occasions where this is simply impossible. Pregnancy is one of those. We all have heard the horror stories of teens who try to handle pregnancy alone—babies end up in dumpsters and teen mothers kill themselves. This is a time when we need you more than ever, and that is when it is so important to be able to open lines of communication so that your teen knows that she *doesn't* have to handle this alone.

Of course, you're going to want to know as quickly as possible if your teenager is pregnant, so you can help her make the right decisions that affect her health and the baby's health.

Because some teenagers won't show any drastic physical changes until late in pregnancy, how can you get your teen to tell you that she is pregnant?

> ***A couple days after my seventeenth birthday, I found out I was pregnant. I was always so careful, but a few times I had sex without a condom, and I guess the rest is history. The first***

person that I went to when I found out was my mom, because I knew she would understand.

SARAH, AGE 17, MONTCLAIR, NEW JERSEY

I asked Sarah why she was so sure that her mom would be so understanding.

I knew because of little things. Like when that terrible story about the prom baby was in the news, my mom didn't say anything like, "That slut—she deserves to be sent away for life," like so many other people were doing. She was more like, "That poor girl—where were her parents? What was so wrong, that she couldn't tell her mother?" I was still a little nervous about the whole thing, but I knew that if my mom could feel for someone she didn't even know she definitely would with me.

SARAH

As much as you think that we don't listen to what you say, we really do—but at times you think we are not. Sarah, and many other teens I have spoken to, make the decision to talk to their parents about tough sex issues based on how their parents reacted to similar situations that didn't have anything to do with them. Your teen needs to get the message that you will be there for her if she needs you, and that you won't flip out and get angry. But you can't wait until some awful thing happens before you find a way to let your kids know how you would treat them if they told you. You need to get that through *now.*

I spoke to many teens—both girls and boys—who told me the main reason they didn't go to their parents was because they were too ashamed or because they were afraid of the reaction.

We have a thousand thoughts flying through our heads. We do not know if you will ever trust us again. We do not know if you will hate us, or just be horribly ashamed, hurt, mad, or appalled. And this is why we are so hesitant about coming to you.

To quell this hesitation, you need to reassure us that your reaction will not be any of the above. By doing that, you open up the gates for us to be truthful.

But what if you do feel ashamed and hurt? What do you do then? Many things that we do hurt you, and if you feel it is important for us to know that, then you should tell us, but in the case of pregnancy, this rule does not apply.

> ***I was really scared to tell my mom and dad that I was pregnant. I held off as long as I could, but when I couldn't anymore my mom went nuts. She kept saying, "How could you do this to***

me?" I was already feeling horrible, and that made me feel tons worse. But I didn' t do anything to her, I only hurt myself.

MARY, AGE 18, CHATTANOOGA, TENNESSEE

As much as Mary's mom was affected by the situation her teen unintentionally forced her into, Mary had too much on her shoulders already to be able to carry her mother's guilt as well. Teens have told me that this is not the time to make things be about yourself: You're not the one who is pregnant. Teens say if you really want to help, it doesn't matter if you truly feel hurt or not, we need you to center all of your attention on us; adding your own feelings will just complicate an already complicated matter.

Another very important thing that teens say you need to remember when dealing with pregnancy is that we need to know that you are not only thinking about the problem, you are also thinking about us. In the case of other issues that we teens face, we're separated enough from our problems that you are able to first concentrate on the issues and then come back to us. But with pregnancy, there is no way to separate us from our problem. We're literally connected to it. And we don't want our problem to separate us from you.

What if you're the parents of sons? Does that mean you don't have to worry about any of this? You may be surprised that there was really no difference between the ways that teenage girls and boys talked about the fear of pregnancy. The same reasons a girl is afraid to tell you that she is pregnant are the same reasons why a boy is afraid to tell you he got someone pregnant.

"I could never tell my mom I got an STD."

A study conducted by the U.S. Department of Health and Human Services reported that, in the United States alone, more than 13 million people contract STDs each year, and more than 65 million have an STD that is incurable. With the discovery of AIDS and other serious sexually transmitted diseases, sexual promiscuity has become a dangerous game to play. And the real danger is when teens don't know there is one. But we are the reapers of the Information Age; how could we not know the dangers? I took the liberty of asking a few teens some questions about what they thought were potential consequences of having sex, and here is what I got. I think you might be surprised.

You can only get AIDS if you are gay.

BEN, AGE 14, LAMONT, KANSAS

The only way that you can get an STD is if you have sex without a condom.

HSU, AGE 17, DUNCAN, ARIZONA

When you are on birth control, you don't have to have sex with a condom because the pill kills STDs.

SALLY, AGE 15, FARMINGTON, CALIFORNIA

Another case where teens "know everything"—and another case where a lot of us are wrong.

Waiting to talk to a teen who you think is "too young do be doing such things" just might be too late. An article posted in *The New York Times* said, "Some studies indicate three-fourths of all girls have had sex during their teenage years, and 15 percent have had four or more partners." Another polling funded by Planned Parenthood found that almost 46 percent of 16-year-olds and 57 percent of 17-year-olds have had sexual intercourse. And with this behavior comes a rise in teen pregnancy and teenage contraction of STDs.

My mom and dad always talked to me about having safe sex, ever since I was like 13. They never tried to scare me and tell stuff that wasn't true, they just told me what can happen if I have sex without a condom, and they spoke to me about different STDs and about AIDS. I have had a few boyfriends since I was 13 and I have had sex, but I would never think about having sex without a condom.

CAROL ANN, AGE 17, COLORADO SPRINGS, COLORADO

Carol Ann's mother spoke to her frankly and truthfully about the potential consequences of sex, something that teens say can greatly increase your chance of getting through.

Most teens look at sex and sexual behavior as all fun and games. The media practically romanticizes sexually deviant behavior. Teens all over the country are getting the wrong message, so it is up to you to give the right one. The teenagers who seemed the most satisfied with their parental conversations about sex said that their parents never told them that sex itself was a bad thing, but that irresponsible sex is.

Before you start talking to your kids about STDs, the first thing you need to do is your own homework. Don't forget, your kids have no shortage of misinformation. They need to know that they can come to you for correct information.

When it comes to STDs, you need to be able to tell us what the different kinds are, what their symptoms are, how they can be spread, and how to prevent them—and this means explaining to us about condoms, and more importantly, how to use them.

I talk to my dad about girls and stuff, and he always tells me to wear a condom, and I do, but a couple of months ago my girlfriend and I had a scare. We went to Planned Parenthood and she took these pills to make sure she wasn't pregnant or anything. They asked me if I knew how to use a condom, and I was like "obviously, you just have to slip it on." But it turns out you have to do other things like leave some room at the top, put on a new one every time you have sex, change it if you have it on too long, and other stuff I never knew.

GARY, AGE 17, TRENTON, NEW JERSEY

A condom is a simple contraption, and it is a highly effective guard against STDs and pregnancy, but only if used *correctly*. Talking to your kids about the proper way to use a condom can be an uncomfortable thing for both of you. But keeping in mind the steps to a successful conversation that we explored in the beginning of the chapter, you will have a much better chance at getting through. Girls have told me that when their boyfriends put on a condom incorrectly they made sure it was on right. So, don't think that just because your teen is a girl she doesn't need to know this information. She does.

Talking to your teens about STDs and their symptoms is a perfect chance to lay the groundwork for making them feel sure that it's okay to come and talk to you about them, whether they have contracted them or are just curious.

My dad has spoken to me a good amount about STDs and the things that happen to you when you get them. He always says to me how important it is to wear a condom, and that I am playing with my life if I don' t use one. But he also says if something happens and I make a mistake and start getting any symptoms, that I should go to him right away. He said he wouldn' t be angry or ashamed, and he wouldn' t tell my mom or anyone else.

Well, I had been with this girl for a couple weeks. We had sex one time without a condom, and it started burning when I peed. I was so embarrassed, but I knew if I told my dad it would get it taken care of and no one would know, so I did. It turned out that I had gonorrhea; I took some antibiotics and it went away in a couple of days. My dad wasn' t mad at me or anything, but he told me I was lucky because my situation could have been 100 times worse. I know I was stupid, and I also know that was the last time I would ever even think about having sex without a condom.

RON, AGE 16, ORGAN, NEW MEXICO

A lot of the teens I spoke to who have (or have had) STDs didn't tell their parents because they were too ashamed or embarrassed. How could they tell you that they think they have an STD, when most of you don't even think they are close to having sex? Because of their embarrassment and the reaction they suspected from you, many of them let their STDs progress and get worse. Ron's dad did the right thing. He reassured him that everything Ron thought he would do would *not* happen if he just told him. This not only allowed Ron to take care of his problem quickly, but it also proved to him that he could trust and confide in his father, something that will improve their overall communication greatly.

"But everybody else is doing it!"

Sometimes it's hard for older teenagers to abstain from sex because they feel like sex equals acceptance. Acceptance by friends, acceptance into adulthood, and even acceptance of ourselves.

Luckily, it is easier for teens to talk to their parents about *this* problem than it is about some others concerning sex—because they know that you will be delighted to hear that they are *not* having sex.

But just because it may be easier for us to talk to you, doesn't mean that we'll do it. Like in most all sex conversations, you will have to initiate this one.

My mom and I were driving in the car a couple of days ago when she said, out of the blue, "You know, it is perfectly okay not to have sex." I haven't had sex yet, and I really don't think that she knew that. The random way she brought it up made

me think that there actually was a problem not having sex. All I said to her was, "Okay." I was sort of feeling uneasy about the fact before, but now even my mom feels bad for me, so I know I'm pathetic.

SANDRA, AGE 17, QUINTER, KANSAS

Sandra's mom didn't feel bad for her that she wasn't having sex—I bet she was thrilled—but all she wanted to get through to her daughter was that she shouldn't feel pressured to have sex just because everyone else has. But her message was destroyed because of poor initiation.

Teens have told me that a better way of initiating the discussion would be to wait until there's an opening. For example, if you're watching a video or a TV show pertaining to sex (something that is not that hard to find these days), you could ask, "So what do you think of that?" This gives your teen an opportunity to express his or her opinion without the conversation getting too personal.

Once you've gotten the conversation started, teens say they'll listen if you discuss your own feelings about sex, making sure that you let us know that you respect our opinions just as much. Maybe you'll say that you personally believe that it is not necessary for kids to be having it at a young age, or that when people choose not to have sex it is their decision and people need to respect it. You can say that making your own choices and not conforming to what everyone else does makes you a stronger person. It's a cliché, but it's true.

Teens don't seem to mind theoretical, third-person conversations like this. They aren't likely to feel threatened if you throw the conversation back and ask if many teens feel that way. By posing the question in that manner, it allows us to express our true thoughts without us feeling vulnerable and attacked. You might actually get the truth out of us for once. You shouldn't ask us personal questions, but sometimes teens say it can help if you become personal yourself—as long as you spare us the grisly details.

> ***This radio commercial came on in the car one day when I was driving with my dad. It was one of those Trojan ones. He asked me if a lot of kids my age have sex. I told him not really, but that kids a year or two older than me do. Then he told me that when he was 17 most of his friends had done a lot more with girls than he did, and he always felt that he was left out. So he ended up going out and doing stuff with girls who he didn't really like. He said he regrets it to this day. That was basically the end of our conversation. I kind of felt the same way he did, and even though I have not spoken to him about it yet, I feel like I could if I wanted to.***
>
> TIM, AGE 15, QUIMBY, MAINE

Some teens say that telling stories about yourself allows us to realize that you were a teen once, too, and you have gone through the same sort of things that we do today. But you should watch out about using this method because some teens will just be repulsed hearing stories about you having sex, and want to run screaming from the room. If you test the waters by slipping in a personal thing here or there and see how we react, you'll know if this technique will work.

Kids also have a lot of peer pressure to accept the prevailing attitudes about sex. I would say this is one of the hardest things to be able to talk about with your parents because it's incredibly personal. But it's an important topic. There are a lot of stereotypes about sex that are not always true from person to person. If your child's point of view is different from those stereotypes, he or she needs to know that that's all right.

There are lots of things your kids may have problems with and want to talk about. Maybe they think they started to have sex too early and now they just want to stop. Maybe they are afraid they cannot please their partner during sex, or they don't feel good about their reasons for having sex. If you can talk to your kids about how they're feeling without telling them they're wrong or bad, then they'll be more willing to come to you with more of their problems and concerns.

"I think I'm gay. Do you hate me?"

Different experts have different opinions on how many people are gay and lesbian. Some say 2 percent, some say 10 or even 15 percent. The point is, it's a lot of people, and it's an important issue. In this day and time, homosexuality is becoming more and more open and more and more a part of society. I don't have to tell you that there are a lot of different views about homosexuality. I know that certain religions—and millions of people around the world—think that it is a horrible thing. But if your teenager is gay and thinks you feel this way, it's going to make for a very difficult life for both you and your child. The question you need to ask yourself is: Do you hate homosexuality more than you love your child? Some teenagers worry about it.

A good friend of mine, Seth, a 17-year-old from New York City, just "came out" to a few of my close friends and me a couple weeks ago. When I asked him if he had told his parents yet, his response was, "Hell, no," so I asked him why.

Seth: I don't know; I just don't feel like I can right now.

Rhett: Why not? Have they said anything that would make you think that they wouldn't like it if you were gay?

Seth: No. Well, not really, neither of them did anything to make me think that, but that's the thing. They haven't said anything that would make me think they were okay with me being gay, either. I'm not afraid of telling my mom, but if I tell her, my dad will find out, and I just don't know how he will react. I know he has a gay friend or two, but it's different—I'm his son, his only son, and he is a pretty rough-around-the-edges guy. I'm going to tell him eventually, but I think I'm going to wait until college. I don't know what he'll think when I tell him. If he is okay with it, that will be great, and if he isn't . . . well . . . then I'll just know he's a bastard.

Seth is scared to tell his dad that he is gay because he doesn't know how he will react. His father never did anything to make him think that he wouldn't be okay with it, but he never said anything to make him feel that he would be okay with it, either; he's said nothing. This is a classic example of what can happen when there is a communication problem. If Seth's dad made it perfectly clear to him that, gay or not, he would love and respect him just the same, Seth would have no problem telling him; but he hasn't. You cannot expect us to be able to guess your reaction about something like this. To us, saying nothing speaks volumes. It tells us that you aren't okay enough with the fact that we could be gay. Your silence begets ours; speak up, so we can, too.

So how to initiate a conversation about homosexuality?

Teens say a good way is to have some kind of reason to bring it up that isn't threatening, for example, after you've watched a TV show that has a gay character with your kids. Ask them how they feel about the character, and then ask them how they feel about homosexuality. If they say they see nothing wrong with it, make sure that they understand that it would be okay if they were gay also. But you have to be careful about how you say this. Teens that I have spoken to said that their parents would say to them something like, "You know it's okay if you're gay." If we happen to be, this comment would make us feel that you are trying to force us to tell you, and things as big as this cannot be forced. They say a better way to approach it is if you say something more like, "You know I love you unconditionally—it wouldn't matter if you were gay, straight, or anything else for that matter." I know this sounds a little sappy, but posing the statement this way won't make us feel like you are trying to pry out a homosexual confession.

What if, when you ask us what we think about homosexuality, we say that we don't like gay people, or that we think homosexuality is wrong? Teens say you need to ask them why they think that, and where they got it from. Then you need to explain that there is nothing wrong with any person's sexual preference, and then talk about being prejudiced, and what it does to the world.

I got that message loud and clear when I was in sixth grade.

Pretty much all throughout middle school, if you didn't like someone or something, you'd call it gay. The word became a substitute for anything considered bad or "uncool." I became so used to it that I started using it all the time, so much that one day I made the mistake of calling something gay in front of my mom. I didn't think twice about what I had said until she said, "How dare you!" She went on to tell me that saying things like that and being prejudiced are the same things that caused the deaths of over 6,000,000 Jews just like me in the Holocaust. She told me that by me saying things like that, I was continuing to allow things like this to happen in the world. As giant as her example was, it blew me away. That was pretty much the last time I ever called something gay.

You don't have to worry—by telling your child that being gay is okay, his or her sexual preference won't suddenly change. Sexual preference is not a choice. It's part of who your child is. You will not make the decision for them. But your input, your understanding—or lack thereof—could make a huge difference in their lives. It's *your* choice whether that difference is negative or positive.

Cracking the Code:

A Mom's View on What a Parent Can Do

"You don't have control over the choices your kids make," Dr. Ellie Taylor told me. "But you have control over being a good parent."

Wow. I'd never heard it said quite like that before. Ellen Taylor, M.D., is a gynecologist in private practice in Baltimore, Maryland, a frequent speaker on a variety of female medical topics, and recently named by *Baltimore Magazine* as one of Baltimore's top doctors. She was talking specifically about the issue of a child who's gay. But she could have been talking about any of the issues surrounding kids and sex, kids and communication.

And in fact we did talk about all of them. I interviewed her and her husband, Dr. Bruce Taylor, together. Bruce T. Taylor, M.D., is the medical director of Sheppard Pratt at Ellicott City, Maryland, a board-certified psychiatrist and Distinguished Fellow of the American Psychiatric Association, whose main practice is with adolescents in both short- and long-term inpatient programs. In a free-ranging conversation that covered all aspects of teen sexuality, teen sexual practices, and teen sexual knowledge, the Taylors, who have four children of their own, kept coming back to the same inescapable answers: honesty, openness, and communication, communication, communication.

Rhett's teenage participants say "don't personalize," and Ellie agreed. "Of course kids don't want you probing into personal details of their lives," she said. "I don't need to know the specifics. It's a turnoff. It would turn me off."

So what do you do if you don't personalize? Ellie suggested "talking in 'ifs.' You don't have to ask your teen, 'Are you having sex with your boyfriend? Are you having promiscuous sex? Did you do it last night? Are you using a condom?' " You can put it in terms of "ifs," such as If you feel pressured to have sex, remember it's not right if it's not okay with you. Remember your friends are not in bed with you. At the end of the day, you're the one you're going to have to answer to. Don't make it an interrogative by saying "If you are having sex, *are* you using a condom?" Instead, give your advice straight away: "If you are having sex, *make sure* you are using a condom."

Most important, the Taylors agree, is regular communication, constant communication. They don't agree with all of Rhett's caveats, though they don't entirely disagree, either.

What about the idea that kids will get turned off if you use anatomically correct language like "penis" and "vagina"?

"Those are the words," Ellie says. "What else are you going to use? If you're uncomfortable using the words, or if it feels like you're forcing them, then there'll be awkwardness. But if you start calling things by their proper names when kids are young, and they grow up hearing them, there shouldn't be any awkwardness."

The Taylors emphasized, over and over, that the important thing is to talk. Should you make sure that it's a safe, short conversation, such as during a car ride? Should you be careful not to call the teen into your turf, so that he doesn't feel too uptight?

Those things are less important than making sure you have the conversation, the Taylors say. If you wait until the right moment, the right moment may never come. And "the right moment" can be as forced and wrong as any other moment, such as "Let's all watch *Sex and the City* together, and maybe we can talk about things they talk about."

Don't put artificial limits on a talk. It doesn't have to be closed-ended. It doesn't have to stick to a predefined agenda. If your teen suddenly opens the door to a marathon, free-flowing discussion about every aspect of sex and sexuality, go with it.

The talks about sex when my parents' generation were talking to my generation were just different. And perhaps the most different thing about them is this: With the possible exception of certain kinds of father-son conversations that I wasn't privy to (and none of my male friends recall having), they weren't about condoms.

Now you can't get away without talking about condoms.

"Remember," the Taylors counsel, "there's no such thing as safe sex. The best you can talk about is safer sex." But that being said, you have to make sure that if—that "I-word" again—your kids are having sex, or thinking about sex, they understand about condoms.

Make sure that they understand that condoms provide a measure of protection against not only pregnancy, but disease. If a girl is on birth control pills, she still needs to make sure that a condom is used when she has sex, because the pill can't protect against disease.

Make sure they understand that you *always* use a condom. Ellie is particularly fervent on this point. "In any relationship that cools off, it's always going to cool off for one partner sooner than for the other. And that partner may go off and have sex with someone else. And is he going to come back and say, 'Honey, we'd better start using condoms, because I'm being unfaithful to you'? Not likely."

Should girls carry condoms, too? Here's a question that never came up when we were kids. But today, the answer is yes. If a girl is going to be sexually active, she needs to know that she can't count on someone else to make sex safer. She has to be the one.

Can parents of boys be a little less vigilant? After all, boys don't get pregnant. And the answer is no, they can't. Disease strikes both genders equally. But not only that, a boy who gets a girl pregnant is just as responsible for the welfare of that baby as she is.

Should parents buy condoms for their kids? There's certainly an argument for it. At least that way you can be sure that your kids have them, even though it doesn't guarantee they'll use them. But for a lot of us it just doesn't feel right. We may not believe that abstinence is the answer to sex education. But we still don't want to be in the position of appearing to encourage our kids to have sex.

"I don't tell parents not to give condoms to their kids," says Bruce. "But I don't encourage it, either."

Maybe the mom who put the condoms in the cookie jar on the kitchen counter has the right idea. It's halfway between.

Do what works for you, which generally means do what's comfortable for you, and then do a little more. And don't ever stop communicating. Use the advice Rhett's teens have given in this chapter on how to make communication less awkward, but if it doesn't quite work for you, or if you can't quite set up those magical stress-free situations, then be awkward, but communicate. As Dr. Waters says, there are worse things than looking like a jerk. Your kids have to know about condoms, and safer sex. They have to know they can come to you with a pregnancy, they can come to you if they think they're gay, they can come to you if they've had sex and didn't like it and wonder if that means there's something wrong with them, they can come to you if they want to have sex and want to be on the pill, or if they don't want to have sex and are feeling peer pressure. If you talk to your kids, you may not reach them with everything you say. But if you don't talk to them, you'll never reach them.

Chapter 4

SELF-EXPRESSION AND PRIVACY

When you think about it, a young child doesn't really have his or her own identity. Everything—the way young children dress, what they eat, who they hang out with, how they brush their hair—is dictated by their parents. Sure, their unique personality shines through on the playground or in their interactions with their friends, but for the most part, a child is someone's son or daughter. Adults' identities, on the other hand, are dictated by no one other than themselves. To travel from boy to man or girl to woman, from an identity that is given to you to one that you create, you must cross a bumpy path of uncertainty: better known as adolescence, the time of self-exploration.

This journey of self-exploration takes teens to scary places like Johnny's basement: once a child's paradise filled with Legos and toy trains, but now more of a den of tempting teenage vices. Things we do in the name of self-exploration, seemingly harmless to us (like coed sleepovers in Johnny's basement) raise red flags for parents. The little girl who once adored ribbons in her hair and frilly dresses one day arrives at the breakfast table with a belly-button ring. The boy who once lived for Little League suddenly wants only to hang out with his friends and goof off on his skateboard. It is a tough job finding yourself—and a lot of us reinvent ourselves several times throughout our teenage years. So even if we sometimes seem malicious or contrary to reason, it's all just part of a process we all go through.

We are only teenagers for a fleeting moment, yet it is one of the most memorable times in people's lives. This is because in these quick years we morph from child to adult, a transformation of amazing proportions. But for us to pass through this period unscathed is easier said than done. You know you can't just sit back and wait for us to emerge from our adolescent cocoon and bloom into a beautiful butterfly—now more than ever we need your perspective to help us through.

Yet here is where things get tricky and family problems arise. How do you safely guide us, when your guidance is what we are trying to separate ourselves from in the first place? As you might have guessed, the teens I interviewed had some thoughts on that question.

HAIR AND CLOTHING

Part of finding yourself is testing and trying new things. One way we do this is by making drastic modifications to our hair and clothing. This is nothing new—I'm sure parents in the 1960s were horrified when their kids came home in tie-dyed shirts and bell-bottom pants. And those parents probably horrified *their* parents when they were teens with the fashions of their day. Still, some adults seem to forget this as soon as they have kids of their own.

"I didn't change my appearance to hurt you."

Part of finding our identity is experimenting with different looks, but sometimes our motivation for a drastic change in appearance is misinterpreted.

> *I was always forced to keep my hair long. Everyone, including my mom and dad, said that if I cut my hair short I would look bad. So I shaved my head, and I think I looked just fine. My*

mom thinks that I did this to hurt her, but if I wanted to hurt her I would burn the house down, not shave my head.

CINDY, AGE 17, WISTER, OKLAHOMA

Many parents look at actions like this as something we are trying to do *to* them. Sometimes they are, but most of the time that is not our motive at all. Most teens say that when they do drastic things like this, they do them simply because they want to, not as some sort of personal stab against you. For that, as Cindy said, we can come up with more creative ideas. Trust me, this is our first chance to express ourselves in this way. We are not about to do something big that we think makes us look stupid just to make you angry.

My mom used to buy me clothes and I had to wear them, end of story. But now I make my own money and can wear what I want. I dress punk—that's what I like. I get flak all the time from my parents telling me I can't go out of the house looking like that. Well, I really don't care what they think.

JAMUL, AGE 15, DELMAR, MARYLAND

The bottom line is, not every drastic change we make to our appearance is because we want to spite our parents. But there are a lot of times when we're rebelling against the rules you've made us obey, but there are also times when we simply want to experiment—to see how we look with that Mohawk, or dressed all in black, or with a nose piercing. So how can you keep your kid from doing radical things like this? There is no cut-and-dried answer to this question, but some teens say you can keep them from rebelling if they have no reason to rebel in the first place.

> *When my mom would buy my clothes, she would bring me to the store with her and let me pick out what I wanted. It didn't matter if I wanted a Batman uniform, she would allow me to buy it. She always let me dress how I wanted. Some of my friends dress differently just because their parents never let them. I dress the way I want to dress, but I guess because my mom never made me wear anything I didn't want, I don't feel like I need to buy a patent-leather jumpsuit just to prove to her that she doesn't have control over what I wear anymore.*
>
> HALEY, AGE 16, NORTH BRANFORD, CONNECTICUT

Allowing us our freedom of expression when we are young will give us no reason to want to rebel when we're older.

"When you criticize the way I look, you're criticizing me."

The truth is that dyeing your hair blue or putting on black eyeliner and a spiked necklace is no big deal; hair grows and makeup and clothing come off. But there is one aspect of this situation that can have a permanent effect, and that is your reaction. Sometimes when we do something drastic, we are looking for a reaction; we are looking to see how you will handle what we have done to ourselves. The way you react and what you say can have a direct effect on your future communication with us.

> *A year ago, I shaved the sides of my head and made a Mohawk. I was in the bathroom for a long time, and then I came downstairs when dinner was ready and sat down. My dad freaked. He was like, "I can't believe you did that; you're grounded forever." My mom had a different reaction. She calmly said she liked my hair how it was, and she wouldn't have changed it. She didn't yell or try to punish me, or anything, she was pretty cool with it.*
>
> HARRISON, AGE 17, RICHLAND, SOUTH CAROLINA

I then asked him what his relationship was like with his mom and dad.

> *My dad is a dick. He only wants what he wants. We don't really talk a lot, and especially not after I gave myself a Mohawk. He didn't talk to me for like 2 weeks. But my mom is pretty chill, I talk to her about stuff. My dad only likes me when I am what he*

wants me to be; my mom might not like what I did, but she was cool with it because I really liked it.

HARRISON

Most kids expect a certain reaction from their parents when they do stuff like Harrison did. If you give us that angry, disgusted reaction, it gives us more reason to want to keep doing these things because we feel like we are making some kind of stand against you. But it's not only that—when you react harshly to a change in our clothing style, makeup, or hair, you feel like you are only passing judgment on our actions, but we don't see it that way. Most teens say that what they choose to show the world is an outward reflection of themselves, so even though you may think you're just hating our choice of clothing, we see it as hating us.

That is why your reaction is so important. You don't have to like what we've done, but we'd like you to accept it as a natural mode of expressing our newfound freedom . . . from you. When you do that, it makes us feel like you understand us better and might cause us to feel more comfortable talking to you about the other tough subjects focused on in this book. This is not only true when we actually do dye our hair purple, but also when we come to you and tell you what we are planning.

The bottom line about it all is this: The way we

communicate about these things, the way we talk to and treat each other, will stay with us long after the Mohawk grows out. So take advantage of these opportunities to build trust instead of waging the war of the wardrobe.

TATTOOING AND PIERCING

Hair and clothing changes, in the grand scheme of things, are not a very big deal. You can call yourself lucky if this is all your teen has done because there are other popular forms of teen self-expression that do not just grow out when you don't want them anymore.

Teens notoriously act on impulse. We can look back and laugh one day about the time we dyed our hair blue, but it's very different with a tattoo or piercing. Generally speaking, these things last forever, the impact of which is hard to grasp for us teens.

My best friend Dave, who is 17, just got a tattoo. It is hard to describe him, but he is anything but an impulsive person; he is very planned and meticulous, almost to the point of being compulsive. So when he came back from the shore one day and said he got a tattoo of Kokopelli on his back, I was shocked. (Why would he want a Native American deity? I have no idea.) I actually liked it, but this was very un-Dave-like behavior. I asked him why he got it and he said, "It was a rainy day, so I wanted to make it exciting." Not exactly the best reason I've ever heard.

The point of this story is, for us teens looking for our identity, this is the time to shine, try new things, and break out of the confines that have we have been placed in. Unfortunately, the result of trying new things could be a Kokopelli on your back for the rest of your life.

I want to get a tattoo so bad, but my mom said if I get one, she will kill me. Whatever—it's not like that is going to stop me. I'm getting one in a couple of days with a friend of mine. We're both getting suns on our lower backs.

HENRY, AGE 16, OVERBROOK, KANSAS

My mom said that I couldn't get my ears pierced because I would look trashy. I got them pierced the next day, and she grounded me. But when I got off my grounding I got them pierced again. Every time she grounds me, I get my ears pierced one more time. I have five now.

KELLY, AGE 15, DENAIR, CALIFORNIA

So how do you talk to your teens about piercing and tattooing in a way that will get them to be reasonable? Should you say "no" and risk them doing it just to defy you, or say "yes" in some kind of attempt at the old "reverse psychology" to trick us into not doing it? Teens say, say it how it is.

> *I told my mom and dad that I was going to get a tattoo when I was 16. I thought it was nice that I even did that. My mom did not like what I said at all; she just went on screaming her head off, "No child of mine is going to ruin himself!" My dad tried to calm down my mom. When he did, he pulled me aside and talked to me. He said he did not want me to get a tattoo, but he knew he could not stop me. He said that before I go do this, I need to remember that a tattoo lasts for life, and that it will just make things harder for me. I asked why. He said that having a tattoo gives off certain signals to the world; people will judge me even before I say a word. He said it's wrong that people do this, but everyone does it. My tattoo would speak certain things about me that I didn't want it to, and it could keep me from getting jobs in the business world. I ended up getting a tattoo anyway, but on a place where no job interviewer would dare looking.*
>
> PONCHO, AGE 18, TERERRO, NEW MEXICO

"No" is an answer that no one wants to hear, but it is a lot more palatable when it is backed with a good reason. A lot of teens won't really pay you much attention if the only reason you don't want them to get a tattoo is because you simply don't want them to. Poncho's dad gave him reasons not to get a tattoo that would directly affect *him,* and he got through.

Some parents feel that there is no need to have this conversation because in most states, kids under 18 cannot get a tattoo or piercing. But as they say, laws are made to be broken, and thousands of teens all over the country make it a job to break this one. It is incredibly easy to purchase a fake ID, or find some unscrupulous piercing and tattoo artist who would be more than willing to do work on a minor. If we really want to get something, we'll find a way. So teens say explaining your reasons and the concept of permanence, instead of just saying "no"—or worse than that, saying nothing—might just keep those earrings out of our noses and tribal deities off our backs.

FRIENDS

Part of the self-discovery process is questioning. Questioning your authority, questioning ourselves, and questioning our friends. They say you can judge a person by the people they surround themselves with, so it would make sense that if you are trying to change yourself, you would need to change your friends also. Not all teens search for new groups, but the ones who do might need some special attention from you. You see, it is quite easy for us teens to get wrapped up in a group that, well, might not be right for us—meaning one involved in drugs or other questionable pursuits. But you might not be able to quickly spot these groups. Teens say that parents often make the mistake of judging a book by its cover.

> ***This year I started to hang out with a new group of friends. My mom and dad think that now I'm like a hoodlum, doing drugs and stuff just because my friends dress differently. The funny thing is they don't even do any drugs, other than smoke cigarettes. They might have black clothing and dyed hair, but they are good people and they're my friends. My parents are so stupid.***
>
> KEARNY, AGE 15, WEBSTER, MISSOURI

"Before you judge my friends, get to know them."

Looks can be deceiving, especially with teens. Black clothes and dyed hair might have spelled trouble in your day, but in ours they don't really spell much at all. These teens are trying to be different, trying to form an identity, not necessarily doing drugs. The only way to really know your teen's friends is to—well, get to know them. It's important to find opportunities to do this because getting to know our friends will indirectly give you a lot of information about us. You really can judge someone by the company he keeps, so get to know our company.

Since it may be hard to truly "know" the kids your teen is spending his time with, how can you know if he is hanging with the right crowd?

> *My mom always complains that she doesn't know any of my friends because I never bring them around the house. Whatever; I don't want to bring my friends around the house. I don't have to, so I won't.*
>
> JEROME, AGE 16, PRINCETON, MAINE

I bounced this interview off of a few teens, and they told me that Jerome probably doesn't want his mom to meet his friends for a reason. Maybe he is afraid that she will judge them before she meets them, like Kearny's parents; maybe he is just afraid that she will get to know them and dislike them anyway; or maybe he just plain doesn't want her to get involved in his social life. But despite our reasons for separating our friends from you, you need to get to know them in some way. To do that, you will need to assuage our fears and somehow get through to us that you won't react the way we think you will.

> *My mom and dad are pretty old-fashioned. I would never have brought my friends to meet them because I know they would hate them. It's not like they are bad kids or anything, it's just they're different, and my parents don't like different. But I*

eventually did bring them over, and my parents were cool with them. I decided to do this because of something that my dad said to me a while ago. We were walking in the street shopping when a group of punky-looking kids walked by us. I thought he would have some comment like, "they're all druggies" or something, but he didn't. He asked me if my friends dressed like that, and I said yes. Then he said he thought it was good that they weren't like everyone else and that he liked that they were being themselves. I don't think he really thought that, but I knew he was trying.

SANYO, AGE 17, DARIEN, CONNECTICUT

Proving to us that you won't be judgmental with our friends might make us a little less apprehensive about letting you meet them. But what should you do if you don't like them *after* you've met them? What then? If you give them a real chance and you still suspect that they are bad kids, you can, of course, tell us that we can't hang around them anymore, but that may not have much effect. Teens can be pretty creative about finding ways to see the people we want. You can force your teens to let you meet their friends, but it is a lot harder to force them to stop being friends. Teens say the best thing you can do in this case is just keep a closer watch on us. Friends have a lot of influence on us, and if that influence is a bad one, you will be able to see the change—but only if you're paying close attention.

"My mom is on my case about the music I listen to. What's up with that?"

Music for many teens is a staple of their existence. And there have always been disputes between parents and teens over exactly what type of music they listen to.

Some of today's most popular music icons may be viewed by some parents as too risqué. So should you really be worried about what type of music your teen listens to? Here's what some of them said.

My mom's all freaked out about the music I listen to. She says it's too angry, and it's the same kind of music those boys in Columbine listened to. I like that kind of music, that's it. I'm not about to go to my high school with a gun because of it. I think she just needs to calm down.

TONY, AGE 16, RAMONA, KANSAS

I don't like any of that pop stuff everybody is into now; I like rap. But my mom is psycho about it. If I buy a rap CD, she'll throw it away. She says it gives bad messages.

RITA, AGE 14, CAROLINE, MARYLAND

Teens say that censoring the type of music they listen to—just like stomping out other forms of expression—will only push you farther away from them because they feel you can't relate. Truthfully, I think you have bigger fish to fry than whether your teen listens to rap. Teens say that even though you shouldn't censor their music, you should know what they are listening to. Since it is a form of expression, you should be aware that sometimes the music we listen to is a reflection of our mood. Teens say that if your kid is listening to demonic and depressing music, you should take extra care to notice what else is going on in your child's life or any drastic changes in behavior.

PRIVACY

Since we feel that we don't normally get a lot of it, privacy is a sacred thing to teenagers, something that we need and want more than anything. But what I have found from my own and other teens' experiences is that parents don't especially like how private teens can be. We sit up in our rooms talking for hours to people you don't know about things you don't know, come down for dinner, rush through monotonous small talk, and then are out the door. This is the normal routine of many teens, and I can understand how it can be frustrating. But it is this frustration that causes a lot of problems.

The other day, I noticed that my diary was not how I left it, and my dad was gone for the weekend, so I knew it was my mom. I asked her about it and she said that she didn't touch it. I knew she was lying to me. She has no right to go through my stuff.

KELLY, AGE 16, ORANGEBURG, SOUTH CAROLINA

Technically, because we're living in your house, you do have a right, but all I can say is it's absolutely, positively guaranteed to piss off your teenager. So if you go through your teen's personal things, you need to realize what you might be doing to your future communication.

Trust is the keystone in any relationship, and breaking that trust comes with serious consequences. I guess in this way, we are pretty hypocritical. We break your trust all of the time, yet for the most part, you keep on giving it back to us, but when you break ours, the repair is much harder. I guess we hold you up to higher standards than ourselves, and as far as we're concerned, the same rules do not apply to us.

If you decide for some reason that you must go through your son's or daughter's personal items, do so at your own risk. If you are found out, communicating with us will be even harder. If we can't trust that you won't go into our rooms and search through our things, then how can we trust you enough to have open communication?

So what do you do if you happen to find something in

your child's room? Well, that all depends on what you find, of course. Your plan of action will be very different with a gun than with a *Playboy.* Teens told me if it is something minor that you are concerned about, you should bring the topic up and give us the heads-up that you are not as clueless as we thought. For more serious finds, teens say you can do one of two things. You could make up a story about how you just "came upon" this or that, or you could just plainly tell them the truth. But if you are going to go for door number one, I would be careful about the story you tell—make sure it is plausible.

My mom came to me one day with pictures of me and my friends drinking and smoking (and not just cigarettes). I got in sooo much trouble. But I also was so pissed that she went through my purse. She told me that she was looking for makeup and she just saw them. I know that is a crock of shit; why would she want any of my makeup? We have totally different tastes. I felt really betrayed, and we didn't talk for a while.

JESSICA, AGE 16, AKRON, OHIO

I asked Jessica if her mother ever gained back her trust.

My mom and I are actually better than we were before now. She made large efforts to show me that she respects my space. Like before she used to clean my room (probably just for the reason of finding something she could use against me), and now she does not even set foot in my room. Seeing the pictures was a shock to her because before that she thought I was this innocent little girl, but now she knows what I do when she is not around. When we talk now about that kind of stuff, it's not like parent-child, it's more real.

JESSICA

Jessica's mom gave a bogus story that Jessica did not believe and lost her daughter's trust. But she was able to gain it back by showing her daughter that she respects her and her privacy. This actually helped their relationship in many ways. So even though teens like Jessica might be furious about the invasion of their privacy, deep down they realize that it is your job to keep us safe.

Cracking the Code:

A Mom's View on What a Parent Can Do

Is there any possible way for kids and parents to be anything but natural adversaries when it comes to privacy? I hope so—and I have come to believe that it is actually possible to get on the same page with our kids.

Kids value their privacy, and that's a good thing. We

should respect the privacy of others. But, they're our kids. We need to know—more than anything else in the world—that they're all right. We don't have to know who they have crushes on, or what they're reading, or even (by the time they're teens) if they're listening to songs with naughty lyrics. We don't have to know the secret thoughts, hopes, dreams, and fantasies that they confide to their diaries, or the socially unacceptable wisecracks they trade back and forth with their friends on the phone. We just have to know they're all right.

So is it ever acceptable to pry, to snoop, to spy? What is the acceptable protocol on this? Is there such a thing?

"You don't ever snoop unless the kid has drawn first blood," says Ruth A. Peters, Ph.D., a psychologist specializing in treating children, adolescents, and families; contributing psychologist for NBC's *Today* show; and author of *Laying Down the Law: The 25 Laws of Parenting to Keep Your Kids on Track, Out of Trouble, and (Pretty Much) Under Control.* "You don't snoop just to snoop. But if you have good reason to believe your kid is doing drugs, or if your kid has been skipping school a lot, then all bets are off."

Her advice would be my advice, too. You want your teenager to survive his teenage years alive—and not having done anything that will irreparably damage his future. The guideline I'd use would be the guideline my rabbi gave me years ago: *Does it matter profoundly?* Maybe the way she wears her hair doesn't. But maybe what she's smoking does.

If you decide that the potential harm is so serious that you *have* to know what your teenager is doing, what do you do? Dr. Peters described clients of hers who installed wire-tapping devices in their attic to bug and tape their kids' phone calls. A friend of mine, after her son went through rehab for a serious drug problem, bought a new "family pet"—a drug-sniffing dog, retired from the DEA. Other families have installed burglar alarm systems—not to catch burglars trying to sneak in, but to catch kids trying to sneak out.

Rhett says if you have to snoop, don't let yourself be caught. Because if you are, it will destroy parent-kid trust forever. Dr. Peters also says don't let yourself be caught, but for a different reason: "Your kids will go even further underground."

Should you confront your kid with wiretapped evidence? Don't be afraid to, says Dr. Peters. Use the "first blood" justification: It's legitimate. "You did this, so I have to do that." But if you can use the knowledge you have to quietly head off trouble, to stop something from happening before it starts, then that may be the way to go.

"You have to use your judgment," she says. "You have to have the guts to go with your gut. And you have to be willing to have your kid get angry if you say no. But," she adds, "you can't say no all the time."

Being a teenager is the dress rehearsal for being an adult. Being the parent of a teenager is the dress rehearsal for being the parent of an adult who earns her own living, doesn't live under the same roof with you, and may be living with someone else, in fact. It's the dress rehearsal for letting go.

You can't say no all the time. You can't say, "Don't go to the prom, don't go to parties after the prom, there may be drinking there." But you can do what a friend of mine did. Her daughter and friends were getting a suite at a hotel for the prom night party. My friend booked a room at the same hotel. "You may not need me. I hope you don't. And I won't interfere unless you do. But I'll be there if you do need me."

Your kids deserve their privacy. They deserve to be allowed to begin the work of creating their own lives. But they have to have lives to create, and that's the line you need to draw.

Does it matter profoundly?

Chapter 5
SCHOOL ISSUES

I am awoken by bloodcurdling screeches from my alarm clock every morning at 6:01 exactly, ripping me from a dream right before it starts to get good. I'm sure it must look pretty humorous, me flopping my hand, fine-motor skills numbed by sleep, in search of the Holy Grail of all buttons: Snooze. I slump back onto my pillow, hoping that I will go back to the dream girl at the ice cream store, but quickly come to the realization that not even in my dreams will *that* happen. I shower, brush, fumble with my clothes, and am out the door at 6:40, waiting for the bus with the millions of other teens across America who are still a little resentful the whole ice cream thing didn't work out. We all pile into the bus we wished wouldn't come, sit back on the seats that have backs at an angle just steep enough to be uncomfortable, and wait for our day to begin. Grades, teachers, college applications, report cards, detention, homework, tests, quizzes, projects, GPAs, SATs, monotony, stress, pressure, and endless deadlines lie in wait at the last stop on the route, ambushing us the second we descend from the bus and enter the esteemed corridors of education, a.k.a. our school. For 12 years *this* is our life. No wonder school has been—and forever will remain—the bane of the teen existence.

It's not that I—and most other teens—hate school or the idea of learning, it's just that we hate the stress that seems to be inextricably bound to it. But the stress of high school and preparing for college is not bound only to us; *you* also seem to get wrapped up in it, which starts a slew of other problems for both sides.

MAKING THE GRADE

There's no way around it: School is all about measuring up. From having the right clothes to making the team, school is one big competition—and I haven't even mentioned academics yet. When it comes to tests, papers, and lab projects, we feel the pressure from all sides—our teachers, our parents, and, yes, even ourselves. Here's what issues came up most for teens I talked to.

"My mom and dad yell at me constantly about my grades."

This seems to be *the* issue that parents have: We, your teens, are not doing as well as you would like. This makes sense. All parents want the best for their kids, and seeing us not getting the grades that will set us off on the road to "the best" is something that a lot of you won't stand for.

> *I don't do very well in school. I normally get one or two Cs and the rest are Bs. Every time I get a report card I get screamed at by my mom and dad, but it's mostly my dad. He just keeps telling me that my grades are "unacceptable" and grounds me for a week. He says that if I don't do better I'll never go anywhere in life.*
>
> David, age 15, Tuscola, Michigan

> *I have taken the SATs a few times, but I still don't have scores high enough to go to the schools I want. I feel bad enough; I don't need my parents yelling about them constantly.*
>
> Gala, age 17, Fair Oaks, California

David's and Gala's parents are just a few of the millions of parents around the country yelling the same speech at their kids. But yelling is normally *not* the parents' first step, it is the culmination of ignored requests and maybe even threats of punishment. So when teens tell me their parents yell about their grades, it tells me that the parents have already gone through the motions, and *still* the teens haven't improved their grades. So, the yelling—and the "unacceptable" grades—continue. Why? I think Lee put it beautifully:

> *I would always get in trouble about my grades. I would sometimes not be allowed out for weeks at a time. I got the same grades (mainly Cs, Bs, and the occasional D) all through high school, until my senior year. I ended that year on the honor roll, with all As and a B-plus. The reason for the change is because I realized that if I did not start doing better, I wouldn't get into any of the colleges that I wanted. It didn't make a difference how many times my mom and dad would yell at me, I started getting good grades because I wanted to, not because my parents did.*
>
> LEE, AGE 19, DARLINGTON, SOUTH CAROLINA

Lee could not be any more right: It really doesn't matter how badly you punish us. The only way we will do well in school is if we want to. On a few occasions, I've often heard teens say they do badly just to spite their parents. (Okay, not our generation's brightest moment, but it happens.) So how do you get your teen to *want* to do well? How can you get us to understand the importance of school? Teens say to have any chance at doing this, it helps to shift gears. The parents who have had the most success stopped yelling and started explaining reality.

> *My mom always yelled at me when my report card came in the mail. But about a month ago, the day came when I knew I would get reamed out again because my grades did not get any better. I stood there as my mom was looking at the report card and got ready for her explosion, but it didn't come. She looked at it for a while and then just handed it back to me. I was so shocked, I said, "That's it?" She said "I guess so," with this sad look on her face. I was relieved that I didn't get punished, but I didn't get it—she should have done at least something to me.*
>
> *That night just she and I were eating dinner, and she said, "You're probably wondering why I didn't punish you," and I nodded. She said that she had given up, and that she wasn't going to yell or punish me because of my grades again. She said she just realized that there is no point to it because no matter how badly she could punish me, it wouldn't be close to how badly I was punishing myself. I had*

no clue what she was talking about, and I gave her a look saying that. She went on, explaining that what I do in school has nothing to do with her, but everything to do with me. She said I have made it clear what my decision is so there was no use trying to change it anymore. I still didn't really understand what she was getting at. She said I obviously didn't mind going to a college below my potential and that clearly I was willing to struggle my whole life having that *fact drag me down. And then she said she was perfectly fine with the choice I had made. Then she just continued to eat, not saying another word. I didn't say anything either, but I understood what she was saying, and she was right. Since then I* have *been working harder, and I have brought up my grades, at least a little.*

JEROME, AGE 16, HAGERSTOWN, MARYLAND

Jerome's mom (and others like her) realized that yelling and punishing her son was getting nowhere. To get through to him, she found a way that really worked.

As much as I'd like to say that's all you need to do, I know with some kids it'll just go in one pierced body part and out the other—until the day your teen looks at where he is and realizes that you were right all along. Opportunities look a lot bigger leaving than coming, but unfortunately some of us don't realize this until we experience it ourselves.

"I try so hard, but I still get in trouble for my grades."

The most any of us can do in life is our best, but sometimes teens say their best is not good enough for their parents.

I try really hard in school, but I only get Cs and Bs. I tell my mom and dad that, but they don't believe me. They yell at me and say they know I can do better if I just try harder, but I really can't.

RACHEL, AGE 16, TRUMBULL, CONNECTICUT

I can understand why Rachel's parents don't believe her. She probably puts a lot of time and effort into other aspects of her life and excels in those areas because of it. So her parents expect that if she put the same effort into school, she would also shine. The truth is we teens have the tendency to say things like this just to get you off our backs; we really could do better but we know you can never ask us to do better than our best. So how can you separate the truth from the lazy? One girl from California said her dad did something with her that leeched out that truth.

My dad really is hard on me about my grades because I don't get good ones. I told him they are as good as I could make them, but he didn't believe me. I was so angry at him that he still got mad at me about my scores. But one day he said that if I could prove to him that I was trying my best, he would get off my back. He said that for the next week I had to show him what my assignments were, do them, and then show them to him. I said no, but then he said that if I wasn't willing to prove it to him then why should he think I was telling the truth, so I agreed. I was forced to do every part of every assignment, even the stuff that my teachers don't go over; it sucked. But it was even worse because I did *do better. So now I'm back to getting in trouble.*

LIANA, AGE 15, DEER PARK, CALIFORNIA

If you berate your teen for not trying hard enough and he really is doing his best, you will just make him feel horrible. After all, hearing that your best isn't good enough is a tough thing to handle—especially coming from your parents. Liana's dad got around that by calling her bluff. He challenged her to show him what she was doing and said they'd decide together if that was really the best she could do. He took the focus off of grades (which sometimes we think we can't really control) and put it on effort (which we can control). No yelling, no unrealistic expectations. Score one point for Dad.

But what if your teen's grades don't improve even after

she dutifully completes every assignment? If your teen really seems to be doing her best but is still getting less-than-stellar grades, what can you do to help?

> *I had to repeat my freshman year because I failed. My dad was so mad at me because he thought I was slacking off, but I really wasn't. I told him that it was just hard for me to understand things sometimes. I kept telling him that, so he eventually had me tested. The tests revealed I have dyslexia. Since then, I have been in special classes where they teach you differently, and I am getting good grades.*
>
> TOFER, AGE 17, NORTH CARROLLTON, MISSISSIPPI

Many parents around the country simply ignore their child's complaints about schoolwork altogether, thinking that they're just being lazy teens. Some of these teens may have learning disabilities, which can be diagnosed and addressed. Just because some of us need to be taught differently than others does not mean that we are stupid. *Not* knowing that we have a problem makes us feel inadequate, which can cause serious self-esteem problems down the line. That's why it is so important to take what we say seriously. You are probably right in thinking that we are not getting the grades we should, but if you don't investigate the reasons, we might never realize our true potential.

CHEATING

The shortest distance between any two points is a straight line. But a lot of the time, standing between a good grade and us is a hopelessly long, difficult, curvy one. So comes a choice: We can either study, research, and take the long path; or if the situation presents itself, we can take a shortcut and cheat. There are very few of us who can actually say we are not guilty of cheating once or twice. It just seems so easy to do it sometimes; why do more work than we have to?

I was caught cheating once in my life; it was when I was in middle school. I forgot that we had this big grammar test in Mr. Pizzo's English class. Realizing I did not have enough time to study in the 3 minutes before class, I quickly jotted down, on my hand, what I needed to know and then went to class. It worked perfectly; when Mr. Pizzo would look away, I would look at my hand; I knew I had aced it. I would have gotten away scot-free, but unfortunately, I was overcome with a bout of stupidity. Believe it or not, as the rest of the class went on, I forgot that I had written anything on my hand, so lo and behold there I was diligently raising my adverb- and preposition-covered hand high to answer a question, when I caught an odd look from another student. By the time I realized what I was doing, it was too late. I was caught. I got a zero on the test, but I think Mr. Pizzo felt so bad for my stupidity that he said that he wouldn't put my cheating on my transcript. He told me that if he did, I would carry it with me for a long time and I would be labeled as a cheater. He went on, saying if I pulled a stunt like this in high school, it would go on my permanent record and it could keep me from getting into college, none of which I realized. (Note to any college admissions officers who happen to pick up this book: Feel free to disregard this confession. I really won't mind . . . really.)

Teens say that it would help them resist cheating if you took the time to discuss with us the repercussions of cheating. Many said they would think twice about cheating if they understood the enormity of the offense.

Of course, there are many teens who know the repercussions of cheating but still decide to go ahead and do it, thinking that flunking a test could be just as bad. When these teens get caught, what are you supposed to do, and how do you keep them from cheating again? Well, teens say that you first need to distinguish between two different types of cheaters. Consider the different motivations behind Klive's and Trisha's cheating:

> *I just hate to do homework and study for tests and stuff. I do listen in class, but I'm not going to work for another 2 hours every day doing stupid busywork. So I cheat sometimes. I got*

caught a couple weeks ago. But I have to cheat or my grades will get worse than they already are.

KLIVE, AGE 16, BISBEE, ARIZONA

I am not a cheater, but now my parents think I am. I got caught cheating on a math test a month or so ago. I was getting As in the class all semester, but I just totally forgot to study. I had to cheat.

TRISHA, AGE 15, ROCKLAND, DELAWARE

I am not going to tell you not to yell at us—we cheated and we should get yelled at and punished, but that only goes so far. What makes a lasting impact with teens is when you go further, and help us solve some of the issues that caused us to cheat in the first place. The difference between Klive and Trisha is in how you can help them. I've spoken to a lot of teens like Klive, and I hate to say it, but many of these kids just don't care—they see cheating as the only way to go. They trap themselves early in the year in a cycle of cheating that is exceptionally hard to break. Most classes are cumulative, so cheating on one test means that you won't know or understand information on the next test, and so on. They go on cheating just to keep up. One thing that has helped kids like this is developing better organization and study skills. If your teenager is perpetually behind, try talking to his school and asking them to work on setting up an organized study schedule so he can break out of the cycle—or better yet, avoid starting it at all.

Teens say you should treat situations like Trisha's differently. She is by no means a serial cheater and fits the breakdown of the most common cheaters: good students who find themselves in tough situations and make the wrong choice. But there may be other factors at play.

I just have so much pressure on me to do well. I want to go to an Ivy League school, but not nearly as much as my mom and dad want me to. I couldn't let one test ruin all of my chances and let down my parents.

JERRY, AGE 17, BELMAR, NEW JERSEY

My son is a good kid but now he might get kicked out of school for taking a teacher's answer key and cheating on a test. I'm not in any way condoning his actions—he made a bad move and should be punished—I just think the school is acting too harshly. I see the work he is doing and what kind of classes he is taking. This kid is trying his hardest to get into the colleges he wants to, and now he may not have the chance. Back when I was in high school everyone was not going to college; the competition that these kids face to be the best is sometimes too much, and I think his school needs to understand that.

NANCY, AGE 47, WASHINGTON HEIGHTS, NEW YORK

Even if your kid isn't shooting for the Ivy League, school is a place of intense stress. And while school has always meant tests, homework, and evaluations, today's students are faced with an increased sense of competitiveness. We are being pushed to succeed by our teachers, our parents, and ourselves.

When you talk to us, try to get at the real reason why we feel we need to cheat. It's most helpful if you tell us that you understand how hard and stressful times are, and then offer some solutions. Maybe we need a tutor, maybe we shouldn't take so many advanced courses. Showing us that you care more about helping us than punishing us can make a big difference.

BULLYING

My initial encounter with bullying came at the first possible opportunity: kindergarten. There was this gang, for lack of a better word, that the "cool" kids were in. They were ruthless in every sense, taking extra cookies, and even having the audacity to stay up and talk during naptime. Okay, maybe they were far from the Crips, but they seemed pretty bad back then. Anyway, their stomping grounds were the playground, where they would make a ritual of tormenting me. This went on for weeks until finally I had enough; I pushed one of the gang members off the swing in a gallant guerilla attack. Now no one was going to mess with me: I had a reputation. I was "Swing Push Godfrey." See, for me, kindergarten was much like prison. I had to give myself a name or somebody else was going to give one to me, and I don't think it would have been nearly as cool as "Swing Push Godfrey."

Well, you know what they say, you learn everything you need to know in kindergarten, and I really think that might be true. You see, high school bullying is not very different (well, minus the cookie stealing and naptime talking). There are always those kids who find pleasure in displaying their supremacy over others—that's just the way it is. I know having the power to put an end to it yourself, being a parent and all, you would do it, but teens across the country told me that is not always the best choice.

> ***When I was in eighth grade, there was this group of kids that would pound on me all the time. I never said anything to anyone because it was my problem. But I came home one day with a bruise on my cheek and my mom flipped and made me tell her who did this to me. The next day when she dropped me off at school, the kids walked by and she screamed at them. I wanted to die; now I would be known as the kid whose*** **mom** ***fights his battles. I had no clue she was going to do that.***
>
> VICTOR, AGE 14, ROXBURY, CONNECTICUT

For many teens like Victor, not fighting your own fights is worse than being fought. If my mom went up to the school bully and said, "Stop beating up on my son Rhett," I would be embarrassed to death. Teens say if you are really worried about your son or daughter, go to their teacher or principal and allow them to deal with the issue.

CHOOSING A COLLEGE

Whether they want their kids to attend their alma mater, be the first in the family to go to college, or choose a college close by so they can live at home, parents often start mapping out their children's post–high school graduation plans years before it's time for the cap and gown. The problem is, these plans often don't match up with what the teens are envisioning for themselves. Of all of the issues that older teens and parents butt heads on, college seems to be one of the most recurrent.

"My parents don't want me to apply to the colleges I want."

Applying to college is a tough process, with the actual application part being the easiest. Before that, we need to decide where we want to go and, more important, where we are *able* to go—and that's where some problems arise. Not only may we not have the grades to get into the school of our dreams, but the school of our dreams may be the school of our parents' nightmares. Frankly, since parents usually foot the tuition bill, your expectations for where we'll go to college become a big part of the equation.

> ***My mom says that if I apply to the schools that I want, I'll never get in. Basically she's saying I'm too stupid. I don't want to go to my safeties, so why waste my time applying?***
>
> **BRAD, AGE 18, SWINK, OKLAHOMA**

A lot of us have eyes that are bigger than our intellects, and because of that, we sometimes shoot too high and end up missing our target altogether. One of my good friends is a singer/actor, and he felt the same way as Brad did. He would settle only for the best schools, and unfortunately, because of that, he ended up having to settle for nothing.

It is a good thing that we have high expectations for college, but when our grades and other nonscholastic credits do not reach the same level, we need to realize that we're setting ourselves up for disappointment. As our parents, you need to find a way to encourage us to keep our head on our shoulders and our goals down to earth, without making us feel like you are saying we're stupid. A girl from Illinois said that her father found a way that worked for her.

I am an intelligent person, but my grades wouldn't tell you that. It's not like I did badly in school—I got Bs and A-minuses, with one C in algebra 2 my junior year, and my SATs were 1260s. I could get into a good amount of colleges with those scores, but none of the ones I wanted to: Yale, Princeton, Brown, Duke, and Johns Hopkins. But I didn't really want to believe that. For a long time, I was planning to apply only *to those schools. My dad came to me one day and said that maybe I should apply to some more reasonable schools, but I said no, I was not going to settle for something less. He said that the problem with those schools is that they have thousands and thousands of applicants, so to weed them down, they look at the things that give a quick and easy assessment of each person—grades and SATs. He said if they took the time to read the rest of everyone's application, the best schools would be filled with more of the best people, like me, and not with simply the best grades. He said I still have a good chance at getting into the schools I want, but I might need to go to a school that I don't like as much, excel, get good grades, and then transfer, which people do all the time. I didn't really like what I was hearing, but it put things in perspective, and it made me feel better that I still had a chance to go where I wanted.*

CORONA, AGE 19, KNOXVILLE, ILLINOIS

By explaining the reality of how college works, by making it clear that we do deserve the best schools, and not by just telling us that we will never get in, you will avoid making us feel that we're stupid. Which is not the case.

"I had no idea my parents couldn't afford to send me to my first-choice college."

I spoke before about how choosing which college we teens get to go to is not solely our choice because you are the ones with the money. But in a lot of cases, money can do more than just involve our parents, it can limit our decisions greatly. These days, it can cost upwards of $140,000 to send one child to a top 4-year college; the median American income is only about $50,000 a year. See the discrepancy? The question is, how do you tell your teen that she can't go to the college that she wants to because *you* don't have the money?

> *I just got my acceptance letters from a bunch of colleges, and I got into the school I wanted to. But that didn't matter because I won't be going there anyway. It turns out my retarded parents didn't put any money aside for me. I hate them. I work so hard for my whole life just so I can go to the college I want, I get in, and now they tell me I can't go.*
>
> CHARLEY, AGE 18, DOUGLAS, MISSOURI

As teens, we're not oblivious—we realize paying the rent or mortgage, buying food and clothing for the family, paying for water, electric, phone service, and all of those other bills that come in each month takes a lot of money. But when our hopes of attending a certain college are suddenly dashed, we—like Charley—feel resentful. We feel like you let us down, and I am sure a lot of *you* feel the same way. One thing that teens say can help is let us know early on. Many parents, like Charley's, will hold off on breaking the news, hoping that their teen won't get accepted into expensive schools, but when we do, telling us seems exponentially worse. There is almost no way to break this easily, but teens say telling us early could make it a bit more palatable.

When I was picking the schools I wanted to apply to, my mom said that she needed to talk with me. She said that she could only afford to pay $5,000 a year. I couldn't believe it, because that meant that I could not go anywhere close to what I wanted. But she said I had options. If I wanted to, I could apply for student loans, and she would help me. She also put a stack of papers on the table and said that she did some research and found tons of scholarship programs, and she would go through them with me and help me fill them out. I was still just so shocked and angry. Taking out loans would mean that I would be paying them off forever, and it is so hard to get scholar-

ships. But I guess I felt a little better that I did *have some options, even if they weren' t the best ones.*

DARIEN, AGE 18, THOMPSON, OHIO

As Darien's mom found, there are ways to pay for school even if you don't have the money. Telling us these options in the same conversation where you tell us that you don't have enough money gives a thin cushion of comfort, and a thin cushion is better than no cushion. Knowing that there is light at the end of the tunnel is comforting, despite how dim that light is.

"It's not fair that my mom is making me go to a school close to home."

Another big reason why parents don't want their teens to go to certain schools is because they think they are too far away and they want their kids closer to home. Some parents will go to great lengths to keep their kids close. A friend of my mom's told me that her son wanted to go to a school in Washington, but *she* didn't want him to be that far away. She let him apply, thinking that he wouldn't get in, but it turned out he did. She found the letter in the mail and threw it away. (See, teens aren't the only ones who do sneaky things!)

Wanting us to be close is not a malicious thing; if anything, it comes from a place of love, but we teens look at it *very* differently.

My mom says that she won't pay for any school that is more than a 3-hour drive. She says that "there are a lot of good schools close to home," but I don't like any of those. She's bribing me, but I can't do anything about it because I can't pay for college myself.

FRAN, AGE 18, OLAMON, MAINE

I realize that college is an opportunity that you, as our parents, allow us to have, and as long as you're paying the tuition bill, you can decide whatever you want. But the teens I've spoken with asked that their parents at least hear them out. They also asked you to think about why you're letting us go to college in the first place. If it is because you want us to go to a school that fits us and where we can best chase our goals and dreams, then by making us stay close to home you may not be allowing us to do that. Of course, if your teen's top reason for choosing a certain college is that she's heard about the legendary parties or because the school is near the beach and she has visions of hanging out in her bathing suit all semester, then all bets are off. But at least hear her out.

As long as your kid's reasons for choosing a college seem legit, then the teens I spoke with say the best way to solve this problem is to compromise; when both you and your teen meet at some sort of a middle ground, everyone wins.

I wanted to go to a school in Florida, but my mom and dad said they weren't going to allow me to go that far away. I wanted to go there not only for the location but because they specialize in the major I wanted. I told them that, but they still said I couldn't go; it was so unfair. I kept asking and pleading, and finally my mom said she would let me go under one circumstance. She would pay for my college, but I had to get a job so I could pay to buy plane tickets to come home twice a month. I got what I wanted, and so did she. I got in, and now I work at a bakery 2 days a week so I can buy plane tickets. It's a pain in the butt, but it's worth it being allowed to be in an environment I love.

ALEXIS, AGE 19, NEW CANAAN, CONNECTICUT

Like Alexis's parents, it's important to keep your mind open enough to have room for us and our wants. And remember: Just because your child is at a school closer to home doesn't necessarily mean you'll see her any more than if she were far away. Lots of kids only come home during long breaks.

PLANNING FOR THE FUTURE

Parents have a tendency to plan our entire lives for us, and some actually see it through. Lots of teens are forced into jobs they don't want to take because their family wanted them to. How did teens report their parents "forced" this to happen? With their very persuasive secret weapon: guilt.

"I don't want the career you picked out for me."

Consider the situations Jake and Greta found themselves in.

> *My dad runs a business. His dream is to have me take it over when I graduate from high school. But it's not my dream—I want to be a musician and go to a conservatory, but I know it would kill him if I told him that.*
>
> JAKE, AGE 16, SUMNER, MISSISSIPPI

> *I am in med school and I hate it. I never really wanted to be a doctor, but my dad wanted me to be one so bad that when I mentioned I might be a little interested, there was no stopping his excitement. I decided I would try it out and if I hated it I would leave. But I can't because my dad would be crushed; he is telling everyone he passes on the street that his daughter is becoming a doctor. He has these shirts and mugs with my school name on them and underneath, "Father of a med student." You see my problem?*
>
> GRETA, AGE 19, CHAMBERS, ARIZONA

When it comes to choosing a career or direction for our lives, it's no surprise that teens explain you have to let us make our own decisions, as hard as that may be. We do want your advice, and we want to talk to you about our options. Deep down we know you can help us do the right thing. But you have to remember that sometimes the apple falls farther from the tree than you would think; something that was right for you may not be right for us. Teens like Jake and Greta are either trying to be nice to their parents or are simply too scared to speak up. If you suspect that maybe we are not happy doing something that you have picked out for us, come to us and ask. Make sure to tell us that you will not be angry if we say we don't like it. If we don't, then talk to us and help us explore our options and—more important—our passions. We want you on our side.

Cracking the Code:

A Mom's View on What a Parent Can Do

I know it's happened to me. One of my kids brings a report card home from school, and suddenly, I feel like Ilse, She-Wolf of the SS.

"What do you mean, a C-minus? What's wrong with

you? Don't tell me you can't do better! No TV for a year! No phone privileges for 10 years!" . . . until even I cringe listening to myself.

And as I listen to myself rampaging on, a small, still voice tells me, "This isn't doing any good."

"It doesn't do any good to yell and punish if kids aren't doing well in school," says Mary Jane Donnelly, a specialist for curriculum and supervision in public education and recently named the New Jersey Educator of the Year by the New Jersey Association for Supervision and Curriculum Development. "It just doesn't work in the long run. The kids . . . especially older kids . . . will just dig in and wait you out, until you get tired of the yelling and punishing, and give up, and they've won."

I thought about the sad truth in that statement: A teen dug in against his parents, instinctively pushing when they pull, saying "No" every time they say "Yes"—and winning means, essentially, not doing well in school.

"Find another approach," Ms. Donnelly advised. "Talk to the school guidance counselor. Talk to somebody. Just don't wear yourself out sticking to one kind of discipline that doesn't work."

Rhett summarizes it really well: "School is all about measuring up." And no one wants to not measure up. Sometimes, as Rhett says, kids do have learning disabilities that haven't been diagnosed. Sometimes they do need a different approach to learning. Those approaches are hard to find, and with today's overhyped focus on doing well on standardized tests, finding new approaches can be even harder. That means you have to work *with* your kids, not stand over them with a ruler.

Work with the kids, work with the school. Talk to guidance counselors, talk to teachers. Remember, if your kid says, "The teacher just doesn't like me," sometimes it's true. Find out. If you involve yourself in healthy ways, it can only help. Healthy ways are talking, listening, trying to understand your teen's problems, and working with your teen to find creative ways to solve problems and connect to schoolwork.

Less than healthy ways include yelling and punishing, paying for grades, and doing kids' homework for them.

The paying for grades issue is a pet peeve of mine. I'm not saying it'll never work. I am saying you should never do it. Kids shouldn't be rewarded with money for good grades. Doing well in school is a kid's responsibility, not work for pay. You can celebrate good grades with a special day, a family outing, a football game, a play, or dinner at a favorite restaurant. But don't pay for grades.

The issue of doing kids' homework for them segues into Rhett's next issue: the problem of cheating.

I was a little uneasy when I saw that Rhett was going to distinguish between two types of cheating. *Cheating is cheating*, was my first response. But then I realized what Rhett was saying was a little different; not two types of cheating, but two types of cheaters. And that made more sense.

But there's only one, and it's not a type. There's only one kid: yours. (Or two, or three, but you get my point.) The issue is helping your kid become the best person he or she can be.

On the issue of cheating, your kids have to know that it's wrong, and the best way to make sure they know that is for you to be a good role model. This is one of those areas where kids will *really* be influenced by your example.

I'd also add to make sure they know what cheating is. Here's what Ms. Donnelly suggested on this issue. "Every high school has a handbook of guidelines and regulations. You don't have to sit down with your teen and go over them every semester, because they don't change, but you should read them yourself, and you should sit down and go over them with your teens when they start high school. They need to know what the grading and testing standards are, and they need to know what the rules are about cheating and plagiarism, what's considered cheating and plagiarism, and what are the penalties?"

And don't forget that the real lessons on what cheating is come from you. If you tell the movie cashier that your 13-year-old is 11 so that he can get into the movies cheaper, the equation is *Money saved:* two dollars. *The lesson given to your child on cheating:* a price you both may be paying back for years to come.

Bullying is one of those issues where kids are going to say, "Leave us alone and let us take care of it." It's an issue they feel as though they ought to be able to handle. I think you need to be more involved than that.

In the first place, you need to know if it's happening. Kids won't necessarily talk about it, but it can affect every aspect of their school experience. You don't want to be yelling at your kid at home for doing poorly, if part of the reason he's doing poorly is bullying. Here are some suggestions on helping your child handle bullying.

Take the problem seriously, but don't overreact. Most of the time, it's best to follow Rhett's advice on this issue. Don't rush off half-cocked and try to fix things.

Listen a lot. Be sympathetic, and let your kids know that you know how they feel. Find out what the kids have already done on their own to deal with the problem. RELATE, the parenting program of the Commonwealth of Australia, advises, "Sometimes children themselves have tried ways of dealing with the problem that could work if consistently employed. Typically, however, they try a tactic once or twice then give up because the bullying persists."

As much as you can, work with your kid. Talk about the

reasons for bullying, and how understanding it can create strategies for dealing with it. Kids—and too many parents—often think there's only one way to handle a bully, and that's to fight him. Even "Swing Push Godfrey's" solution wasn't necessarily the only one.

Ultimately, if the bullying entails really serious forms of intimidation or harassment, you do have to get involved. You don't necessarily have to march down to the schoolyard, but you can make sure the teacher, principal, and school guidance counselor know about the problem. Schools are much more aware of bullying as a serious issue than they were when we were kids, and much more likely to take steps.

Finally, college. A 1999 survey by the U.S. Department of Education asked teenagers to list the top pressures they face. Thirteen percent said it was the pressure to be sexually active, 19 percent said the pressure to use drugs or alcohol, 29 percent said the pressure to "fit in."

Those weren't the top pressure issues. Above them, with 32 percent, was getting into college. And the pressure kids felt most—44 percent of them—was the pressure to get good grades.

Thirty-two percent felt their top pressure was getting into college. That's more than the total students who *went* to college in my day (25 percent in the late 1960s, according to the National Center for Education Statistics).

The pressure is intense on kids these days. Parents are fighting to get their kids into the right nursery schools, and obsessing about whether not making it into the most prestigious preschool will ruin their chances of getting into the best colleges. The range of things that kids have to know today is dizzying (try helping your teen with her computer science homework).

Ms. Donnelly says, "There needs to be more career education in the schools. Kids shouldn't be starting college with no idea of what they're going to be doing in life. Internship programs, shadowing programs, some schools have them, some don't. But there have to be more of them. Parents should work with the schools, and encourage the schools to have more career education. And they can do more on their own, too, talking to their kids about possible careers, taking them to see what people do."

This was really interesting to me. I went to college in the 1960s, at a time when nobody was thinking about preparing for a career. I designed my own major. I studied whatever I took a fancy to. And when I graduated, without any idea of what I was going to do with myself other than a vague fantasy that someone ought to make me an ambassador to somewhere, I kind of wandered into a job in banking, which I was lucky enough to love and to then turn into a career.

I've had real doubts about the value of my education,

though my professor friends tell me that it gave me the flexibility of mind to take advantage of the opportunities I did have.

But things are different today. They're harder. Kids have to face more pressure. They have to be smarter, and they have to be more focused. Ms. Donnelly's advice makes a lot of sense.

Rhett and I are going through the college hunt now. I've encouraged him to aim high—it never makes sense to sell yourself short. But we both know that there are kids with better grades and better SATs. What should we look at for backup schools? He knows he wants a school with a real campus, and he wants it to be in the Northeast; that covers a lot of territory.

A college professor friend suggested, "Talk to young people who are working in the field he wants to go into. Where did they go? What schools have internship programs that serve as a conduit to jobs in those fields? The college I teach in regularly places a lot of graduates in network and local TV. Other colleges have other specialties."

But Rhett really doesn't know what he wants to do. Is he doomed? Does he have to map out his life before he ever gets to college?

"Of course not," my professor friend says. "You still have time. He needs to go to a school that has a strong core liberal arts program so that he'll have a good grounding when he does decide on a direction—and if that means transferring, he'll have solid credits to transfer."

Finally, I believe that kids should have a financial stake in their education—even if you can afford to pay your kids' entire tuition, the young adults should be making their contribution as well. I believe it should be 25 percent of the total cost of tuition. They can do that by getting scholarships, getting loans, finishing college in 3 years, or working. But they should be doing it.

Chapter 6
MONEY

Money is unique among the other topics in this book, but only because it's so ordinary. You may worry every day about your kids doing drugs or having sex, but you don't actually talk about it every day. Those talks may be difficult or intense, but they do not come up very frequently. Talks about choosing a college, or divorce and remarriage, will only come up when those events occur. Money, on the other hand, is a topic that comes up almost every day as long as your teenager is living under your roof. While talks about money are not as intense as the others, how we deal with money can influence almost every aspect of our lives.

With that in mind, you probably already can see that teens aren't expecting the same kind of sensitive treatment that they're asking for in talks about sex and drugs. Money is generally not a hard topic for kids to talk about with their parents or one that teens have a problem asking their parents questions about. The strange thing is, with difficult subjects like sex and drugs, teens probably feel like they know more than their parents do. But with the very ordinary topic of money, teens usually feel that their parents actually *do* know more than they do.

We also know that our parents *have* more money than we do, and that our parents are an important source, if not the only source, of our own funds. So talking about money isn't a problem, but *how* we talk about it certainly can be.

While your teens want to hear from you on the subject of money, they may not want to hear exactly what you want to say. In fact, quite often what you want to say may be the direct opposite of what we want to hear.

Even if your message is going to be hard for us to hear, there are ways to get yourself heard. In this chapter, I'll share the approaches teens say have worked with them. I'll also share the most frequently mentioned communication problems so that you can try to avoid them the next time you need to discuss money with your teen.

WHEN YOUR TEEN ASKS YOU FOR MONEY

Let's be honest. When it comes to money, you've got all the power. Until we have part-time jobs, we are entirely dependent on you to provide us with funds. So when you want to discuss money with us, you've automatically got a receptive audience. And when we need to discuss money with you, we're well aware that the ball is entirely in your court. Sometimes, though, being reminded of that every time we need a few bucks can seem humiliating.

"Can we talk about this some other time?"

Probably the most common problem I have heard from teens with regard to money talks is that parents respond to a request for money with one of their famous "value of money" speeches. This is pretty much guaranteed to be unproductive, according to the kids I've interviewed.

> ***Once my dad says "No," I've gotten all the answer I needed to hear. I mean, I understand that I need to conserve my money and blah blah blah, but it's not exactly the answer to my question. If that was what I'd wanted to hear, I would have asked.***
>
> **BEV, AGE 13, MANKATO, MINNESOTA**

I guess it makes sense when you think about it: If you say yes to the money request, your teen is already thinking about how to spend that money and isn't paying attention. And if you say no, your teen will immediately turn off, because her motive was just to get money from you, not to listen to your speech. "No," as far as she is concerned, is either the end of the conversation or the beginning of a negotiation, but the only subject of interest to her at that moment is, "Do I get the money or not?"

I ask my mom for money whenever I go out and chill with my friends. I don't have a job, so if she doesn't give me money I can't do anything. But it's all good because she rarely says no to me when I ask. But what she does is gives me the money and then rambles on, talking to me about being responsible with my money, and on and on; I could probably repeat the entire thing word for word by now.

NAOMI, AGE 16, SUN VALLEY, IDAHO

Does this seem selfish or shortsighted on the part of your teen? I asked that same question of Bev, who we heard from earlier.

Look, I don't mean I don't care about the value of money, or that I don't want to know what my parents can teach me about it. I just don't want to hear it right then.

BEV

Naomi was a little more cynical.

They say time is money, and I'm living proof of it. I guess I figure out what my time is worth, and listening to the responsible money lecture is what I pay for getting to go out with my friends.

NAOMI

The "value of money" conversation *is* an important one, but it doesn't help if you are speaking to someone who is not listening. Teens have told me that when they had conversations with their parents about money and handling it responsibly outside of the context of asking for money, things tended to go more smoothly.

"Just because I handle things differently, it doesn't mean I'm wrong."

This has got to be the number-one thing we hate to hear. I'll bet when you were a teenager, you had to listen to your dad talking about how he had to deliver newspapers every day, and somehow he ended by walking uphill both ways. And, let me guess, there was probably snow on the ground, and, if you were really lucky, this all took place in Siberia, where the dictator had outlawed shoes. I'll bet you never liked hearing those stories about how his life was sooooo much harder than yours, and kids tell me they feel the same way as you probably did. (All that I can hope for is that in your stories, you at least had socks for your Siberian paper route.)

The bottom line is, sayings like, "Back when I was your age . . ." have probably turned off kids since cavemen were complaining about how they didn't have fire when they were caveboys. We know things were different then, and even though your point is no doubt important, teens tell me they just don't think that stuff is relevant to them in today's world.

I like to spend my money on things that I like to buy, but some of the things that I buy my dad thinks are unnecessary. He always talks to me about how I don't know what money really is, and all about how when he was a kid, he had to leave high school to get a job to support his family. I understand that he went through rough times when he was a kid, but luckily I have grown up differently, and I don't have to work a job in high school. I'm not him, and even though I am not using my money the same way that he did, that doesn't mean that I am wrong because of it.

DALE, AGE 17, WASHINGTON, D.C.

All I want is for my Mom to remember that I'm an individual, not some kind of clone of her. She is always comparing me against her, but as much as she tries, I will never be her. I am me, as stupid as that sounds, and she needs to understand that.

BARB, AGE 13, DAYTON, OHIO

I wish my Dad wouldn't keep judging me compared to what he was doing when he was my age. In the first place, I don't think he even remembers what he was doing when he was my age—partly because no one could be as perfect as that, so he's gotta be "remembering" a little off.

STEVEN, AGE 15, GILBERT, ARIZONA

The best idea that came from teenagers on this situation was the way this father handled it. Michael's dad was supportive and helpful but let him figure out things for himself, which he found to be the best way to learn.

Sometimes my dad sits down with me and asks me what I'm spending my money on. At first I thought it was because he wanted to make sure I wasn't spending it on drugs, and maybe that was part of it. But he always seems interested, and he never says, "That's dumb," or "That's not worth it." The funny thing is, he sort of doesn't have to. I used to find myself looking at him for his reaction, trying to read something on his face, and sometimes just a raised eyebrow would get me thinking "Hey. Maybe this isn't the smartest way to be spending my money."

MICHAEL, AGE 17, DURHAM, NORTH CAROLINA

"If I listen closely, maybe I can turn No into Yes."

The next most common breakdown is when you say no but don't mean it. This leads to a lot of talks that parents may think are good conversations, but where teenagers are really more focused on getting some money out of you than listening for the moral of your story. Basically, if your kid knows all she has to do is listen to a lecture, nod her head, and agree with you to get money, she'll do it.

Whenever I ask my mom for money she always says no. But then if I come back about 5 minutes later and ask again, she gives me the money speech, and at the end of it I shake my head, and tell her, "Yes, I do understand," and she gives me the money. I don't think what I am doing is a bad thing—we both got what we wanted. I got money, and she got to explain to me the value of money for the 400th time.

RAMAN, AGE 15, GRAND RAPIDS, MICHIGAN

"I never thought of it that way."

If your money conversation starts to sound monotonous to you, then you can amplify that by 100 and that's how it feels to us.

Sometimes it doesn't take much of a change to get your teen listening, at least a little.

I asked my dad if I could have some money to go to the mall. He gave me the money, but I could tell he was mad because he gave me money the day before and I had already spent it all. I was just waiting for him to get mad enough to give me a lecture on being responsible with my money, but he didn't. He said, "Next time when you ask for money, I won't be able to give it to you. When I get my paycheck I am going to go out and spend it all on new clothes and tools—oh yeah, and you are going to have to forget about eating for a while." I kinda laughed at what he said, but I guess he's right, that is what I do.

MAGGIE, AGE 16, JANESVILLE, ILLINOIS

So, it can happen. Maggie's dad broke the monotony of the "value of money speech" with a little humor and increased his chance of catching Maggie's attention. That helped him get his point through.

"Is this REALLY about the money, or something else?"

Here's another problem I've come across, not only through interviews, but also through my own experience. Parents tend to bring money issues into conversations as a façade for totally unrelated problems.

I am what some would call a candy connoisseur. It would be hard to find a candy out there that I have not tried once or twice. I have a passion for sugar.

My mom strongly dislikes the amount of candy I eat and constantly badgers me about it. I know that she does not want me to eat it for a slew of reasons concerning my health, but instead she, as a last-ditch effort, tried to discourage me from eating candy by making it a money issue. I'd heard it often enough that I started thinking about how much money I actually *do* spend on candy during an average week, and the truth is, even though I consume an inhuman amount, I do not spend an exorbitant amount. Candy just doesn't cost that much.

So it is not the money that my mom really gets mad about, it is the fact that I am eating candy, ruining my teeth, doing all sorts of bad things to my digestive system and blood sugar, and ingesting enough artificial color and flavor to turn my skin blue.

So why doesn't she just say that? Maybe it's just easier to use money as an excuse for all kinds of underlying problems that are more emotionally charged.

> *My mom is always all over me about the amount of time I spend on the Internet, and how it's costing us all this money. I never thought it cost all that much money to be on the Internet. Then, when we got a cable modem, she kept saying the same old thing, so I pointed out to her that with a cable modem you're always connected to the Internet and it doesn't make any difference at all how much time I spend on it; it always just costs the same amount.*
>
> *At that point I think that she realized that it really was not because of money that she did not want me to be on the Internet. She then went on to tell me the reasons why she actually did not want me on so much. I'm not saying that I necessarily liked her reasons, but I understood now why she hated me being on so much.*
>
> MOIRA, AGE 13, BURLINGTON, VERMONT

A variation on this theme is when parents will give their teens financial support only as long as they are hanging out with people the parents approve of. Again, it's not so much about the money, it's about something else that is difficult for the parent and child to talk about.

> *My dad gives me money every week for things that I need to buy or do. It has not been a problem for him to do this for me, but then all of a sudden last weekend, he got some power trip. I told him that I was going to go out with a friend and I needed money, and he asked what friend I was going out with. It turned out that he did not like the friend that I was going out with so he told me that he was not going to give me the money. But if I went out with somebody else he would. He was trying to bribe me!*
>
> GILFORD, AGE 17, SOUTH BEACH, FLORIDA

I presented Gilford's problem to a small group of online teens from different parts of the country to see what they had to say about it. Present were: Mandy, age 14, Boulder, Colorado; Jessica, age 16, Salt Lake City, Utah; Jose, age 16, Boston, Massachusetts; and Tolay, age 15, Little Rock, Arkansas.

Tolay: That kid is right, his father is trying to bribe him.

Jessica: Wait, but hold on, I'm not saying this is how I feel but maybe the father has a right to do that. I mean it is his money; he can use it any way he wants.

Tolay: Not to bribe.

Jessica: Well, it is still his money.

Jose: If the dad did not want his son going out with that kid, he should say that, he shouldn't say that he wouldn't pay for him. Because the truth is the dad just doesn't like the friend of his son's. It wouldn't matter whose money he was using, the father wouldn't like his son to go out with this kid.

Tolay: Yeah, but like I said before it doesn't change the fact the father is using the giving of money to his son to have power over him and his relationships, and that's not right.

Mandy: My mom hated this boy that I was dating, and whenever I would ask if I could go out with him she'd try to quickly put together some type of family reunion, make some excuse why I couldn't see him.

Tolay: Well, that's doing the same thing, just not with money. If one of my parents hated someone I was hanging around with or someone that I was dating, I'd want them to tell me that, not to bribe me with some power trip. I'm not saying that I won't hang out with or date the person that they don't like, but if they just tell me and don't do some sneaky thing, I might think about what they have to say.

Jessica: Yeah, I guess so.

Most kids do feel that just because their parents hold the money, it doesn't give them the right to use it as a weapon. Like Tolay said, teens believe that if a parent does not like something that you are doing, they should tell you why they do not like what you are doing—or just tell you that you can't do it—instead of doing what feels like financial blackmail. That way what you actually want to say can be heard, not just the fact that you won't give your teen money for something that you don't agree with.

DISCUSSING FAMILY FINANCES

There's usually a lot of secrecy around the family finances. In fact, I'd say about three out of four of the kids I talked with said they had no clue about their family's money situation. Maybe their parents thought it was none of their kids' business. Maybe they thought they were keeping them from worrying too much, or that they wouldn't understand or didn't care. But that's not what kids tell me—they do want to know what's going on. Here are some things they'd like to know.

"How can we learn about money if it's all a secret?"

My teacher asked my English class to raise their hands if they knew how much money their parents made. Out of about 15 people, 2 raised their hands. And just like some of the other topics in this book, when parents keep secrets from their kids, other problems arise.

> ***I really have no idea how much dough my dad makes. It's not like I wouldn't like to know—I ask him sometimes but he always says he won't tell me. I think he doesn't want to tell me because he thinks that I'll get depressed or something that we don't have enough money.***
>
> **John, age 16, Tarlton, Ohio**

John has no clue about his family's finances, yet he says that his family is probably having financial difficulties. It might seem odd to you, but when you think about it, his assumption makes perfect sense. If you ask a friend of yours about her health and she doesn't want to tell you, you will automatically assume that something is wrong—or else that friend would have no problem telling you. The same thing happened here; John assumed the worst because he thought that his father was hiding something from him by keeping quiet.

What I have found over and over again is that when something is not discussed with teens, they will create their own story to explain it—and the explanation they create may be far from the truth and generally much worse than the truth. And that can be dangerous. All John's father had to do to avoid this problem was to tell him about the financial situation of the family, even if the situation was bad.

"Even if it's bad, it's good to know what's going on."

The truth is that sometimes families really do have serious financial woes, and that can create what is maybe the hardest money conversation to have with your teen. There are a lot of emotions flying through the air in a conversation like that, but your approach can make a big difference in your teen's reaction to the news.

First, as scary as your financial situation may seem, teens say that it's probably best to limit the conversation to the facts as they currently are. Here's an example of a financial discussion where that didn't happen—and the resulting fallout.

> ***My mom gets a little crazy when she is having money problems, and when the market started going down and everyone was losing money she came to me and my little sister and told***

us that we were basically going to be destitute. She started talking about losing the house, and the mortgage being foreclosed, and that we'd all be living in a one-bedroom apartment. That turned out not to be the case, but it took us a long time to realize that. I was kind of mad at her because she freaked us out for basically nothing.

JASON, AGE 16, WALLAND, TENNESSEE

Jason ended up being scared about something that he did not have to get very frightened about. Even if his mother truthfully thought that they were going to be broke, there are better ways to break the news than to freak everybody out. Se-shu's mom took a more reasonable approach.

My mom came to me one day and said that she needed to talk to me about the money situation. She told me that these will be rough times and that she needed my help around the house taking care of my little sister because she was going to have to be working more hours for a while, but that we will get through this no matter what. I was a little scared, of course, but the fact that my mom was acting calm and collected made me feel similarly.

Then she sat down and showed me how much money we owed, and it seemed like an awful lot to me. She told me about how we'd gotten in this situation, insurance and stuff—

I didn't really follow too much of it. But she showed me how much she'd be able to make by working the extra hours, and we could be out of debt in 3 months, and then I felt pretty good. I told her it was no problem and that I'd do my part to help out.

SE-SHU, AGE 15, MONROE, LOUISIANA

Se-shu's mom didn't lie and say that everything was all right; she told her daughter the truth. She also didn't scare her half to death and tell her, "You better get the refrigerator box out of the garage because we're going to live on the streets!"

The teens I've talked with said that it is always better to tell the truth even if it is bad because no one likes to hear, "Surprise, we have no money!" My friend's mom was dating this guy that had money coming out of his ears. I mean like when she was having a bad day at work, he'd run out and buy her a mink coat. Pretty sweet. Then one day his credit card got rejected, the next day his car was repossessed, and eventually he lost his house. Needless to say my friend—and his mom—were completely shocked. That's an extreme case, but Mr. Money Bags was obviously keeping a lot of secrets that got him in deep trouble. So the real trick is to find the right proportion between telling too much and telling too little.

I would say we're not so interested in knowing every dip and rise in the stock market, but if you are truly frightened, it is better to tell us what is going on. Again, though, try to remain calm because we will be gauging our reaction based on yours.

But what do you do if there is actually a serious problem and there is no way out of it? Many of the teens that I have interviewed told me that it is comforting when their parents share the plan they have to rectify the situation.

> *My dad came to me one morning and told me that, as I knew, we were having money problems and that they had become more serious. He went on to say that things were going to change, and that we were going to file for bankruptcy, and that we also might have to downsize into another house. Of course this was a huge shock to me, and I was devastated, but it helped a little that my dad seemed to have the situation under control and knew what to do, and that he explained it all to me. Talking about downsizing to a smaller house was scary, but at least I knew that bankruptcy didn't mean we would be sleeping in the street.*
>
> BILL, AGE 16, ELLSWORTH, KANSAS

Sometimes the truth will be scary, but there are always ways to soften the blow. And that way, as I have seen from Bill's story and many others, is not to just tell your teens that we have no more money, period, end of story, you figure out the rest.

Other times it is impossible to prevent your kids from

reacting strongly to hearing information concerning serious money problems in the household.

> *My mom told me that we were in a lot of debt and that if we did not pay it back soon that there was a good chance that we could lose our house. I was scared, and I broke down and started crying and screaming. My mom tried to console me but there was nothing she could say. I ran out of the house. I guess she could have tried to stop me, but I guess she knew that I needed some time. The next day when I was calmer we talked again, and she explained what we were going to do, and now that I had time to cool off it was easier to take in the whole thing.*
>
> ELAINE, AGE 12, YONKERS, NEW YORK

I have found out over many interviews that this isn't an uncommon reaction. Sometimes when the tensions got too high concerning a serious money problem, it worked out better when the parent took some time to let things cool off and came back to the conversation a couple hours or even days later.

"It's not my fault, so why should I suffer?"

> *My mom told me that we were having financial troubles and she needed me to cut down on my spending.*
>
> PAUL, AGE 16, AUSTIN, TEXAS

Through my interviews I have found out that this is a very common request made by parents who are going through financial troubles. It would seem like a simple enough request, but it didn't quite work that way with Paul.

> *I really do feel bad that we are having money problems, but you know what? That is not my fault; it is the fault of my parents for not making enough money. So why should I get penalized and not be able to go out and do fun things?*
>
> PAUL

This is pretty extreme, and most kids I've talked to wouldn't react that way. In fact, when I showed this interview to other kids, the most common response was "Who does he think he is?"

But I have also found that since parents are the bread-winners, when they do not come through with funds, some-times kids can be a little resentful. Those responses are going to happen, but according to my fellow teens, there are things that you can do to prevent them.

> *I was pretty pissed that my Dad told me that I could not go to the movies anymore because he got fired from his job and that he did not have the money for me to do certain things. But*

after a while my dad, my mom, and I had a conversation about our financial situation, and they explained that we were a family and that we had to get through these rough times as a family. They knew that it sucked for me not being able to do all the things that I wanted, but as a family member I had to contribute toward helping, not hindering, the process of getting out of the financial situation that we were in. I'm still pretty mad, but I understand where my mom and dad are coming from, and it helped a lot that they realized how I was feeling.

BRENDAN, AGE 13, GREENVILLE, NORTH CAROLINA

By explaining that the family had to work together to get through the situation, Brendan's parents cut down on the feelings of resentment that he was having. The important thing to remember is to explain everything fully because if you omit, there is room for interpretation, and where there is room for interpretation there is room for misunderstandings.

When the whole family works together on a problem, it's easier to handle. But can you see why Bob was a little "teed off" at his dad?

It was fine when my Dad told me that we were having money problems and that he needed me to cut down on things that I buy and do. But then he went and bought $300 worth of golf *clubs. How can he tell me to cut down on what I buy, and at the same time keep spending money haphazardly?*

I talked to my mom about it and she told me, "Dad still needs to network and make connections to get into a better situation in the business world." That makes sense, I guess, but if we're having financial problems, can't he network with his old clubs?

BOB, AGE 17, RED RIVER, NEW MEXICO

"The worst is moving."

One of the worst things for a kid to handle when a family has money problems is the announcement that you're going to have to move. It is one thing telling your teen that he has to cut back on what he spends, but it is a whole different story telling your kids that you have to sell the house. To them, this means that the world as they know it is going to be torn up from underneath them and there is nothing that they can do about it. This is hard news to hear no matter how you break it. Teens I have talked to who have endured such situations have told me that most of the conversation felt like this: "Kids, we are going to have to move out of the place that you have grown up in, the place where you have built yourself a life, but it's no big deal, don't worry."

You may not say it that way, but we'll hear it that way. It is important to keep this in mind during your conversation because you'll have a better chance at softening the blow.

My mom and dad sat me down about 4 months ago and told me that because of money problems we will have to move out of our house. They went on to tell me that my dad got a job offer in New Jersey, and that will be where we are going to move. I lived in Texas for my entire life, and I hated the fact that now I had to leave. I tried to fight it, but they said I had no choice, we had to leave. It was a very hard thing for me, with the move and all, and my friends threw me a surprise going-away party, which only made me sadder. My parents allowed me to do all of the things that I needed to do before I left, and they tried to be compassionate regarding the pain that I was experiencing. My mom and dad promised me that we would come back at least three times a year so I could see my friends. This was not a very big consolation, but it helped a little. It did not turn out as badly as I thought. I have made new friends now, but I still think that the move was the hardest thing I have ever done in my life.

FRIEDA, AGE 17, BOONTON, NEW JERSEY

What helped Frieda was not the way her parents broke the news to her about moving. They could have set up the most comfortable, seemingly pain-free environment for the talk, and it would have made no difference. To Frieda, the only thing that would have helped would be not to go, a wish that was impossible to grant.

What her parents did right was simply to understand how hard it was for her. They gave her compassion, and they gave her room to express her feelings. They showed her that they cared about her feelings, and they didn't expect her to just suck it up, and accept it. By doing that, her parents slowed down the speed of the emotional roller coaster that Frieda was forced to ride on.

Some parents might feel that there is nothing that they can do because they are the ones who caused this problem, but that's not the whole story. If I have learned anything from writing this book it would be that showing understanding can be one of the most helpful things you can do, especially at a time when your teen feels alone with her emotions.

"When our lives change, we want to be heard."

Here is another issue that does not directly have to do with financial troubles, but more to do with financial changes. I have a very good friend whose father was a vice president of a company, and he obviously was making a pretty good amount of money. After a while, he grew tired of his job and realized that he wanted to look into something that would actually stimulate him. It turned out that there was a tiny restaurant in town that had gone out of business, and he was thinking of buying it and opening up his own restaurant, which had always been a dream of his. Before he made this decision, he had to think over some major aspects of it, and the biggest one was the money issue. In the beginning, this business venture would cut his annual income almost in half.

I set up a roundtable discussion on the Internet and invited kids around the country to talk to my friend whose father was planning to open the restaurant: Present at this discussion were: Frank, age 17, Chester, New Jersey (my friend in the story); Mischa, age 14, Greenwich, Connecticut; Kalona, age 16, Portland, Maine; and Tom, age 16, Manhattan, New York.

Frank: It would be so selfish of my dad if he quits his job to open up this tiny restaurant.

Tom: Why?

Frank: Because if he decides that he wants to change his job and lose tons of money, fine. But why do I have to suffer for it in the long run?

Tom: Yeah, that does suck, man.

Mischa: Wait, you think that he's being selfish; I think it is you.

Frank: ?

Mischa: You love your dad, right?

Frank: Yeah.

Mischa: Well, if you love him, you should support him.

Kalona: But wait a sec, his dad is going to change Frank's entire way of life because he is deciding to quit a perfectly good job to open up some dinky restaurant. That's not fair.

Frank: Thank you. At least someone sees what's going on.

Kalona: You're welcome.

Tom: Well, what did your dad say to you when he told you about the restaurant?

Frank: He asked me what I thought about it, and I told him I think it would be the single dumbest thing he could do.

Tom: But he asked you your opinion.

Kalona: He should ask Frank's opinion; he is part of the family.

Tom: But he didn't have to. Your dad's choices might affect your life, but he got you where you are now and if he wants he can take it away.

Mischa: I agree.

Frank: Well, I don't.

Tom: Look Frank, I understand that this whole thing sucks for you, but do you really want your dad to suffer in a job that he hates, just so you can continue doing whatever it is you do?

Frank: I don't know. We need to talk about it more, but I think he is making a mistake.

This type of situation may be more difficult for teens to understand because the parent *chose* to do this—the issue isn't being forced on the family through a firing or a declining economy. Frank has a point; it does suck for him that because of his father's decision, his monetary life will be changed for the worse. But does Frank really have any say in his dad's decision? Should he have a say?

Teens themselves are going to disagree on this. But the one thing all of my online interviewees did agree on: If Frank's dad didn't want his opinion, he shouldn't have asked for it. They're saying that if you want to involve your teens in your decision-making process, then be open to what they say. But if you are set on what you are going to do, then make sure your teen knows that he has no choice in the matter.

There are some kids who've made it clear to me that they think they come first. But I believe—and so do most kids I spoke with—that a family is a family. That comes with unconditional support, and that support goes both ways. If you as the parent decide to make a decision that we might not necessarily like, we can voice our opinions and our complaints, but then we need to come back to the place of support. And we do understand that, if you give us a little time to adjust.

SPENDING MONEY: YOURS AND OURS

We have a lot to learn about money. And we'll make some mistakes. We'll also learn better if you can help us when we screw up and acknowledge when we're doing things well. Either way, when we can talk together about the rules, we'll all be better off.

"Oops! How much did you say that was?"

> *One day, I called up one of those psychic hotlines. It turned out to be a lot of fun, so I did it like five times over 2 weeks. What I didn't know was that the calls were costing $3 per minute. By the time Mom got the bill, I racked up $450; boy was she pissed! She made me get a job at a café in my town. It took me about a month to pay it off, but I have been working there ever since.*
>
> STACY, AGE 13, HOOKER, NEBRASKA

Okay, so sometimes we do flat-out dumb things. And it only makes sense that we have to find a way to help pay back our parents for these kinds of mistakes. Just give us a chance to earn back the money—and your trust.

"Hey, that's MY money!"

It's one thing when teens are asking for money from their parents. It's another thing entirely when you are dictating how we spend the money we've earned.

> *During the summer I mow lawns for people around my town. On a good week I normally pull in about $250. My mom told me that I have to put half of that money in the bank for college, and take off another 5 percent and give that to charity. How can she tell me what to do with my money? I'm not making more than a couple thousand, so let me spend it on the stuff that I want. That's why I got a job in the first place.*
>
> JACK, AGE 17, PINEHURST, OREGON

What I have found from many other teens is that if you want your teen to put money in for college, charity, or any other thing, you need to discuss it beforehand so when the exciting first paycheck comes through, you do not have a sudden conversation about how he has to give some of it away.

I told my mom that I wanted to get a part-time job. She was happy that I was getting one, but she told me that some of the money that I was getting had to go toward college. I immediately said no, it was my money. Then my mom explained that college is an important thing and that I had no choice whether or not I gave money toward it. Together we figured out a percentage, and eventually settled on 35 percent. So now whenever I get my paycheck I automatically take out 35 percent.

SUE, AGE 15, OOLOGAH, OKLAHOMA

Even though Sue did not like that money was being taken out of her paycheck, she knew she had to do it. Her mother gave her no choice; she was going to do it. Giving no choice might seem restrictive, but from what I have found, sometimes it is better to set down the ground rules so that your teen knows what she *can* fight about and what is non-negotiable.

Cracking the Code:

A Mom's View on What a Parent Can Do

I've worked one-on-one as a financial counselor with thousands of families and sold nearly one million copies of my books on teaching financial responsibility. I've met families from every walk of life, every social situation and financial position—from those in the throes of bankruptcy to multi-millionaires trying to teach their children the work ethic despite bloated trust funds waiting for them.

So I know that teenagers' first-level thoughts are, well, the same as everyone else's, actually, when it comes to money. Wouldn't it be nice to have as much of it as possible, and be able to spend it on whatever we want?

It's certainly no surprise that Rhett's respondents, when they think about money, think first about how to get it from their parents. And I like what Rhett found out about this: Make sure you know the times when your money conversations will fall on deaf ears, and when your advice has a chance of getting through. I'll only add a few words on what you need to say when you can get through. The basic message you give to a teenager is the same as the message you give to a younger child or a preteen: *This is the way we do things.*

You give that message by repetition, by amplification when there's a window of opportunity, and by example.

There are four possible transactions involving money. You can:

- Get it
- Spend it

- Save it
- Share it

Your kids need to know that all four transactions must be integrated into a healthy concept of money dynamics. Getting it means, primarily, earning it. The only money you can be sure of is what you earn yourself; ultimately, you'll never feel good about your relationship to money if the core of it is not what you earn yourself.

Spending it doesn't exist in isolation, and this is the key point here. Spending has to be done, and planned, in the context of what you earn, what you commit to saving, and what you commit to sharing (i.e., giving to charity).

I believe in starting as young as possible to teach children the connection between value given and value received, with kids' allowance tied to the chores they do. By their midteens, I advocate that kids be off an allowance completely and earning all their own spending money.

I also believe in starting young to teach kids how to budget money, and how to save it. That's why I created the Jar System, where kids divide up all their earnings and gifts into categories (literally using jars, for younger kids): Quick Cash, which they can spend on anything they want (subject to family rules about junk food, war toys, etc.); Medium-Term Savings, where they learn to save money over a period of time for something that they can't afford; Long-Term Savings, which become part of their contribution to their college education; and Charity, where kids begin to learn that they're part of a larger community, and they have a responsibility to be good citizens of that community. Charity actually comes first: I believe kids should take 10 percent off the top of whatever they earn for the charity jar, and then divide up the rest between the other jars. The habit of sharing, of remembering the less fortunate, is truly one that has to be ingrained young.

Actually, the younger you start teaching all of these lessons, the better; it's easier to work with little kids because they've developed fewer bad habits, and you're dealing with smaller sums of money. It's like potty training—the younger you start, the quicker they'll learn, and the less messy it'll be. But it's never too late to start. The important thing is, at whatever point you do start, stay on message from there on. And it can be done. Kids like to have money, but they like to be responsible, too, and they like to be asked—and expected—to be responsible, even if they don't always show it.

The message teenagers most need to learn is: Money is Finite.

Finite is a difficult concept for teenagers. They think they're going to live forever, they think there's nothing they don't know, and they think there always will somehow be enough money for the things they want.

The first step in teaching Finite is getting your teenagers involved in family budgeting and bill paying. It's the basics, and it's the real thing. This is what we have, this is where it has to go. Are we paying for something on installments? Mortgage? Car payments? Credit card bills? This is how much we're paying off on the principal, this is how much we pay in interest.

The next step is working with your teenager on his own budget.

A teen should be moving, step by step, toward financial independence. That means taking responsibility for his own expenses: clothing, school supplies, etc. Your teen should have a budget and buy his own supplies out of it.

If your teen looks at the budget and says, "Are you kidding? That's not going to pay for one Fubu sweatsuit, to say nothing of the safari outback jacket I was just heading out to buy," then it's time for a serious talk about Need versus Want.

Your responsibility is to take care of the basics: underwear, pants, shirts, shoes, a winter coat, a suit, whatever the basics are for your family's lifestyle. You aren't responsible for upgrading any of those basics to an expensive brand name or the latest fashion statement. You pay for needs; your teen pays for wants.

Teach your teen to shop for sales. Those $120 sneakers don't have to cost $120, and they aren't better if you pay more money for them. Teach her about searching for bargains online, about outlet stores, about "recycled fashions." You can make a deal with her as an incentive: If she finds an item on sale, you'll split the difference with her.

Another way of gradually moving your teen from childhood to adulthood, from dependence to responsibility, is to gradually give her responsibility for her own money by sharing that responsibility at first. When you give your teen the money for her own expenses—for 3 or 4 months at first, then 6 months, then a year—put it into a dual checking account (one that will need both your signature and hers). Then give her a prepaid card that she'll be responsible for, with a finite amount of money she can draw against.

As a proud mother, and as a professional advice-giver about money, you know darn well I wasn't going to let my children grow up without a healthy dose of financial education. But even I was surprised to see how strongly this kind of approach affected Rhett.

Rhett's a typical, frustrating teenager. He'd forget his head if it wasn't attached to him, and since his wallet and cell phone aren't attached to him, he's as likely as not to walk out of the house without them. I've never quite been able to convince him that candy is a want, and not a need. He drives me as crazy as any teenager drives any parent. But at the risk of embarrassing my son in his own book, I have to say that I have never known someone with such an unswerving grasp of values and ethics.

Picture this: Five-year-old Rhett offers 16 cents of his allowance money to help a poor woman in front of us at the grocery store pay for her oranges. When the store clerk told him he didn't have to do that, he said, "It's my money. This is my quick cash. I work for it, and I get to spend it any way I want to."

The woman was a little taken aback, too, but Rhett assured her, "These are the rules in life—didn't you read my mother's book?" (He's since found out that this is not a societal requirement, but at 5, Moms encompass a large part of one's world.) "I'm helping out somebody who needs it, and sometime when I need help, there'll be someone to help me. That's what you're supposed to do."

Or imagine what I felt when 7-year-old Rhett helped me explain the concept of work-for-pay allowance for kids on the Oprah show, and explained that it wasn't prorated. If he didn't do all his chores, he didn't get any allowance.

Oprah interrupted him, saying, "But that's ridiculous; that's not fair. You should be able to do some work and get some money."

Rhett explained patiently, "But that's not the way it is. No work, no pay."

And believe it or not, he didn't outgrow this attitude. Just a few weeks ago, I overheard him talking to a friend who had saved $5,000 from summer and after-school jobs and was planning on buying a new car. "You mean after you give 10 percent of it to charity," Rhett said.

"It's my money," his friend said. "No way."

Rhett said matter-of-factly. "Yea, it's your money, but it's your world, too. You have the ability to give so you've got a responsibility. Ten percent goes to charity."

Unintentionally eavesdropping, my heart swelled.

With a lot of talking, the right kind of direction, and an insistence on obeying our family's values from an early age, the lessons of financial responsibility have actually hit home. They can hit home with your teenager, too.

Chapter 7

DIVORCE AND REMARRIAGE

I was at a party the other day and somehow the topic of divorce came up. My friends started going around the room, saying how many times their mom or dad got divorced, until it came to this one kid who was an acquaintance of most of us but whom we didn't know well. He said that his parents had been happily married for 30 years. Most of our jaws dropped in amazement—not in a congratulatory type of way, but almost with disgust. That probably seems weird, but I think because of all we've all been through, we have lost faith in the bond of marriage itself. So when we heard of a happy one, we almost felt bad for that kid, thinking that he must be in some sort of denial because his parents *can't* be happy.

When I talked with teens across the country, I found that while many value and believe in successful marriages, many also take a practical view of marriage. Countless teens told me that they believe their parents have stayed together for the wrong reasons. And many of them—including myself—believe that sometimes divorce is the most productive thing two unhappily married people can do. Still, though we might understand the reasons for divorce on a purely objective level, that doesn't mean that when it happens to us it makes it any easier. Many—if not most—of the teens I heard from didn't think their parents understood their concerns and fears.

> *I think my parents are getting a divorce, but I'm not sure. Every time I try to talk to them about their fighting they always tell me not to worry about it because it has nothing to do with me. But I think it does.*
>
> ALLISON, AGE 14, NETAWAKA, KANSAS

Children are obviously part of the family structure, but when it comes to divorce, many teens say they are looked upon as superfluous parties. After having witnessed two failed marriages occur in my own home, I understand how intense divorce can be for everyone involved. But as much pain, suffering, and confusion as there is on the part of you and your spouse, there is an equal amount on the part of your child. Tons of the teens I've spoken with say this is a reality that often gets lost on parents too wrapped up in their own struggle.

WHEN PARENTS FIGHT

I understand that fighting is an impossible aspect of divorce to get around. When two people are having trouble with their relationship, they fight; it's just the way things go. Some parents believe that their fighting only involves them and really does not affect their teen very much. However, teens I interviewed virtually all had a universal response to the question, "What was the hardest aspect of the divorce for you to deal with?" It was, "The fighting."

"We feel helpless when our house becomes a battleground."

So much for Home Sweet Home. When parents fight, they're more than likely going to fight in the home, which means that we are going to see and hear it. From personal experience, I can tell you that at times, the house can seem like a verbal boxing ring, with both parents as constant opponents (except for the fact that there is no referee to call blows below the belt).

I remember when I would hear my stepdad and mom

fighting when I was a kid. I was only about 9 years old at the time, and it ripped me apart to see my mom yelling and crying, mainly because I felt helpless. I could do nothing to help the situation; all I could do was sit back and watch the deterioration of a relationship that I had more than a little vested interest in. Parental fighting in general has a bigger effect on us than you would imagine.

I would hide in my room when my mom and dad would fight. I could not keep from hearing them hollering back and forth anymore. I didn't think it was weird that they fought all the time; I just thought that that was something that all parents did.

JESS, AGE 14, MANTER, KANSAS

I would hear plates and other stuff breaking downstairs when my parents got into their big fights. My pop would be yelling, and my mom would be crying, or sometimes it was the other way around. I just tried to chill with my friends out of the house as much as I could, because I never knew when they would blow up again.

GREG, AGE 17, GEORGETOWN, DELAWARE

The simple solution, of course, would be not to fight while the kids are around, but I realize that that's easier said than done—you both live there. It is impossible to totally avoid fighting in the home, but what is not impossible is to avoid *some* fighting in the home.

> *Sometimes when my mom and dad would start to fight, they would go outside. I think they would do it so me and my little brother couldn't hear them screaming at each other. They didn't go outside every time they would fight, but when they did, I didn't have to hear all the fighting, so it made it easier on us.*
>
> MOLLY, AGE 16, OCATE, NEW MEXICO

But what other teens like Molly told me was that just because they couldn't hear or see the fighting, the tension in the house afterward could be just as bad. Avoiding fighting in the home can help, but the teens I spoke with conceded that it was only a temporary solution to a much bigger problem.

"We know you're fighting, so why won't you tell us what's going on?"

I know that you understand that fighting affects your kids greatly, but since you can't avoid the fighting, is there anything that you can really do? You might feel just as hopeless trying to console your kids as we do trying to understand the freight train of fighting that is ripping through our lives. The good news is, teens say that there is a lot a parent can do to alleviate the situation, at least a little. Let's first take a look at some of the problems we face when parents don't talk about their fights.

> *Things were kinda different around my house between my mom and dad about a year ago, and I didn't know what it was. One day I walked into my parents' room because I heard my mom crying. When I went in she stopped crying right away and told me that everything was fine. I thought that she was dying or something because I would see her crying after that, all of the time, but she kept telling me that things were okay. Well, that was a lie. Things were not okay—my parents got a divorce a couple months later.*
>
> SCOTT, AGE 14, HARTLY, DELAWARE

Earlier, I talked about the feeling of helplessness that most teens experience when their parents are considering a divorce. The reason for this is because it seems that teens are constantly put on the sidelines except we're forced to go through all of the emotions that you do, whether we want to or not, because we *are* members of the household. So not filling us in about the fights that we are witnessing makes us feel even more helpless in an already helpless situation. In a time when we need more support than ever, if you can't come to us to talk, we feel that, in turn, we cannot go to you.

Consider the following story from 18-year-old Gary. Though he finally had to confront his parents to get them to explain what was going on, he felt better when he finally got some sort of an explanation.

> *There was this one huge fight between my parents. They would fight a lot, but this one was intense. I was only 12 years old at the time and I came downstairs crying and asked them to stop. I think they realized what their constant fighting was doing to me because they stopped fighting right away, sat me down, and apologized for all of what was going on. Then they told me why they were fighting. They said that right now they were having problems with their relationship, that they loved each other and me very much, and that they were trying to work things out between them. They did not tell me exactly why they were so mad at each other all of the time but it made me feel better that they did still love each other, and that they were trying to fix things.*
>
> GARY, AGE 18, LA PLACE, ILLINOIS

"Without any information, I'll assume the worst."

We're not stupid. We teens pay attention and know when our parents are having problems, even if we don't know the severity. This becomes a problem because of a phenomenon about teens that many parents don't seem to realize. We, in general, are sensationalists. We'll leap to the worst possible explanation for something when we're not given the information to accurately interpret events. So when we hear all of this fighting, a lot of thoughts fly through our minds, and we often come up with explanations that in most cases are worse than what is actually going on.

My mom and dad fight with each other a lot of the time. Last week they were fighting real bad and my dad left the house for a couple of hours. I was so sad because I thought they were getting a divorce, but a few days later my mom told me that she and dad were just fighting, and nothing like that was going to happen.

SHALIYA, AGE 12, UNICOI, TENNESSEE

My mom and dad would have really bad fights. One day my mom threw something at my dad when they were fighting and he got a cut on his forehead. I was too scared to go downstairs and see what was going on, so I just hid in the bathroom. I thought that my dad was trying to kill her and she was trying to defend herself. I thought that for months until I finally talked to my mom about it. I guess it was stupid that I thought that.

JAMIE, AGE 14, STRINGTOWN, OKLAHOMA

It was not stupid that Jamie thought that, and it was not stupid that Shaliya thought her parents were going to get divorced. They knew what they saw and heard and they jumped to conclusions. Without any solid information to explain what is really going on, we teens will create our own stories that, in turn, become our own realities.

"We don't need all the details, but give us something."

The teens I have talked with are begging to know what is going on when they hear their parents arguing. But then we encounter another problem. How can you tell us what is going on without freaking us out more than we already are? To answer this question, I first had to find out what it was that teens wanted to know about your fights. The answer that I got was a pretty unreasonable one: *everything.* Your kids have said that they want to be filled in, but how much should you fill them in?

In some cases, at least, teens may not really want what they ask for.

> ***I would ask what my mom and dad were fighting about all the time, and they would always answer me with some fake little thing like, "We are just having some issues now." I had a real talk with my mom and asked her to stop telling me the same stupid thing and tell me the truth, so she did. She told me that my father was married before and that he had two other children and that because they were asking for money was the***

reason that she and my dad were fighting. I never thought that I was going to hear that. *I was happy that she told me the truth for once, but that was just all too much then.*

James, age 15, Stanton, Ohio

Some teens have told me that sometimes the truth can be more painful than the stories we make up for ourselves when divorce is concerned. And if pain is the thing that you are attempting to quell, then telling your teen what he wants to hear is sometimes *not* the best idea. The truth is always a good thing, but the timing of delivery can make the difference between disaster and success.

One thing that many teens say has worked for them is when their parents gave them little pieces of meat without giving them the whole steak. In other words, they were given enough information to somewhat satiate their appetite for knowledge, but not enough to freak them out.

After my mom and dad started fighting all the time, I thought they were going to get a divorce, and I asked them if they were. They said no. So now whenever they have their big fights, one of them comes to my room and talks to me. They say things like, "Don't worry about it. I know it sounded bad, but we were just fighting because your mother is afraid that my job is not the best for me as far as money is concerned." I ask them more questions and for the most part they get answered. I can tell I am not getting the whole story, but I am glad that they are telling me at least part of what's going on, so I know they are not going to get divorced or anything.

HANK, AGE 16, MANHATTAN, NEW YORK

An important thing to remember about the issue of fighting is that I got a wide range of responses from teens. For some teens, telling them everything (if "everything" is not a complete and utter shocker) worked, and for some it didn't. For some teens just telling them very broad reasons for fighting, like Gary's parents did, will suffice. Different teens were okay with different levels of talking, so it would seem that in the end, it is up to you to know which level is appropriate for us. Keep in mind that teens have told me over and over that the biggest, most solvable part of their parents' fighting is their feelings of helplessness—feeling like they are outsiders in their own home, looking in. So no matter what level you choose, we teens will be grateful that you're talking to us.

"If you don't talk to me, then I must be the reason you're fighting."

Many teens tell me that they believe they're a major reason why their parents have split up.

My parents always get in my face about staying out late. It's not my choice, my friends just go out late. So when I go home, my mom and dad usually yell at me, but then one of them will say something the other one doesn't think is the right thing to say, and they start screaming at each other. It's good for me because I'm not the one getting yelled at anymore, but I feel bad that I cause my parents to fight all the time. But I feel extra bad because I think all of the fights that I cause might be the reason they are getting a divorce.

STACY, AGE 15, DENVILLE, NEW JERSEY

I can drive now, but I don't have enough money saved up to buy my own car, so I have to use my parents'. I normally ask my dad and he says no, so then I ask my mom and she usually says yes. I feel crappy because this always starts big fights between the two of them, and now my dad's moved out.

MAX, AGE 17, EMPIRE, CALIFORNIA

Guilt is a very powerful emotion. So when your teen is feeling unbelievably guilty about something that he should not (like Max and Stacy), it is up to you to exonerate him. Teens like the ones above have told me that the easiest way to handle this problem is by talking to them and explaining the *real* reasons for your split. That way you can prevent your teen from ever feeling guilty about your divorce in the first place.

BREAKING THE NEWS

"Honey, do you mind passing me the butter . . . oh, and I am getting a divorce from your father."

If breaking the news about your divorce were as easy as that, we would have no problems, but telling your teen that you are going to get a divorce is a much harder thing to do. We know it's hard for you, but we get slammed in the face with information that will change the rest of our life, and on top of that, we can't do anything about it. When talking to teens, I tried to dig for good ways to have this conversation. But the problem was, I couldn't find any. I found that all parents can do in this situation is minimize the shocker that you are about to drop on your teen.

"Give me some warning before you drop the bomb."

Teens told me that being caught off guard made getting the news about their parents' divorce even worse. Think of it this way: By the time you and your spouse have decided to get a divorce, you've probably both been thinking about it for months, if not years. But to a teen, the news can be a complete surprise, and he can feel blindsided if he hasn't been prepared ahead of time about what could happen.

I found out about my mom and dad's divorce when they called me downstairs one day. I knew something was up because they never just call me downstairs. I thought that it was probably something about my grades because I knew I did not do too well that semester and my report card was coming in soon. They just sat me down and told me. I could not believe it. I knew they were fighting more often than usual, but I never thought that they would ever *get a divorce. I was really sad, but also pretty pissed that they just dumped this on me. I had no idea that this was going to happen.*

RIANA, AGE 15, SMYRNA, DELAWARE

While it's impossible to make this conversation pain-free, Claude's parents helped him by not keeping him in the dark about what was going to happen:

Both my mom and dad had talks with me months before they actually decided to get a divorce. They would tell me that they thought divorce might be a good possibility. I was not happy at all that they thought that, but when they actually told me that it was going to happen, I was expecting it, so it did not come as a surprise or anything.

CLAUDE, AGE 16, CUTLER, CALIFORNIA

While Claude certainly wasn't happy about the news, at least he was *prepared* for it, which helped him begin to accept it.

"Don't give me false hope about your separation."

Often before couples get divorced, they separate as a last-ditch effort to salvage their relationship. Teens say that if this happens in their families, what they most want is for their parents to be honest about what the separation means and how it will affect the family.

After my dad left, I would ask my mom every day when he was going to come back and live with us because I hated not seeing them together. All that my mom kept telling me was that he would come back soon and that things would be like they always were. He did come back, but only so he could get all of his stuff. She lied to me—things did not go back like they were before.

AVERY, AGE 13, BENSON, ARIZONA

Separation between parents can be a torturous process. And all too often I would get responses like the one on page 247, of parents giving false hope to their kid, only to have him get crushed when things did not turn out how he expected them to. Many teens have told me that you don't have to be afraid of telling the truth when they ask you if you and your spouse will get back together. Even though you may feel that holding back will keep them from getting hurt, you are just causing false expectations that will make the truth even harder to hear in the long run. Teens have told me repeatedly that being truthful when faced with questions about the future of your separation is the best thing to do. Even if you yourself don't know whether you'll ever get back together, you need to tell us that—the more we know, the easier it will be.

When my mom and dad got separated I was living with my dad. The first day after my mom left I asked him if they were going to get back together. He told me that they were trying to fix things and he hoped they would get back together, but he didn't know. I asked him every day and he would tell me basically the same thing, but he would add some stuff about the conversations they had together that day and things like that. After the first week of my mom living out of the house, I asked my dad what was going on with them. He told me that, at this point, he did not think that he and my mom were ever going to be together again. I was very sad when he told me that because I wanted more than anything for my parents to be together, but looking back on it I was glad that he told me the truth about what was happening between them, so I did not have to keep guessing and driving myself crazy.

Jose, age 16, Pecos, New Mexico

THE AFTERMATH

Long after the ink has dried on our parents' divorce papers, we still struggle with how to adapt to the new situations we find ourselves in. And even if the divorce was amicable, you may not realize that your teen might not be feeling the same way.

"How could you do this to me?"

Many teens have told me they are angry with their parents for getting divorced and for the impact it will have on their lives.

I am so mad at my mom and dad that they had to act like little kids about their relationship. Because they could not figure out things between themselves, I have to move to a different town and leave my friends.

Lillian, age 16, Quincy, Ohio

I was beyond pissed that my parents were getting divorced. Now I don't even have a home—I have to go back and forth between two half-homes.

CHANG-LE, AGE 16, PAINESVILLE, OHIO

I have spoken to many teens like Lillian and Chang-Le who feel like their parents' divorce is something that was done to them. But teens have also told me that when their parents explain the reasons for separating or getting a divorce, they feel less angry. Now, at least, they understand that their parents' separation was in fact not a malicious action against them.

"Don't make me choose sides."

There comes a time when fighting—especially pre-divorce fighting—goes beyond just fighting and turns into a much bigger issue, one where teens are forced into incredibly uncomfortable positions. Not by their own actions, not by the situation, but by *you!*

My mom's and dad's fights would normally end with one of them leaving. Whoever stayed would come up to my room and complain to me about the other. They would try to prove to me that they were right about a fight that I had no clue about. They would go on and on bashing each other, saying how this one did this, and this one cheated with this, and that one never did that. Hearing all of these things and seeing my parents act like little kids made me want to jump out of my own skin.

Lori, age 17, Quinton, Oklahoma

I was originally amazed by these horror stories, but after conducting more and more interviews, situations like Lori's became nothing out of the ordinary. I'm not sure what parents hope to gain by telling their kids all of the sordid details about their relationship, but teens have told me that forcing us to choose sides can be one of the most painful and counterproductive things you can do as a parent going through a divorce.

My parents' divorce was pretty ugly; we had a whole custody battle and everything. The thing was, after they had their fights they separately would come to me and tell me all of the things that would make me hate the other one. My dad told me that my mom was having an affair for the past 3 years, and then my mom told me the only reason why she had an affair was because my dad hits her. They were trying to get me to hate the other so I would side with them, but how was I supposed to handle the things that they were telling me? It's my mom and dad, not two candy bars.

Kyle, age 17, Vanleer, Tennessee

How could he choose? The answer is he couldn't, but I found some situations where if the teen couldn't, the parent would make him.

My mom and dad always tried to make me take their side when they would have fights. When I'd take my dad's side it would be great with him; he would take me out to dinners, and games, and other things like that. But with my mom it would be horrible; she'd yell at me all the time over stupid stuff. It would be totally different when I took her side in their fights—then she would be great to me and my dad would be the mean one. It was like I was being punished by the parent I was not taking sides with.

Joey, age 15, Redwood, Mississippi

I heard many stories like this one, with a lot of small variations. Some parents would try to entice their kids over to their side through the giving of presents; others, like Joey's parents above, used punishment. No matter what tactics parents used, teens told me they just made matters worse for them. Now, not only do they have to worry about the fighting around the house, they have to worry about facing repercussions if they take sides.

When it comes to making a kid choose one parent over the other, the teenagers I heard from spoke in one voice, loud and clear: "DON'T DO IT!" Don't try to make us choose sides. Don't try to turn us against another parent. When you do this, it makes us uncomfortable, and you risk cutting yourself off as someone that we feel we can go to—something that I am sure you don't want to do.

"I feel like a spy."

Many teens have told me that in joint custody situations, their parents' only contact with each other is when the child travels back and forth between each of their residences. This would not be a problem by itself, but teens have told me one does arise when parents probe them for information about the situation of the other spouse. When you do that, we feel like you are turning us into spies, infiltrating enemy territory and relaying information to you, a situation that puts us in a very uncomfortable position.

My parents had a very bad divorce, and now they never talk to each other. Under court order I have to spend a week out of every month at my dad's house and the rest at my mom's. Whenever I go to my dad's, he always slips in the, "So, how's your mother doing?" question, then the, "and her boyfriend?" line, and on and on. My mom is no better; usually the second I walk in the door she is dying for me to tell her information about my dad. I tell them what they want to know, but I feel horrible doing it because I feel like I am betraying each of them.

FRIEDA, AGE 17, TREVETTE, MAINE

As you can see from my interviews, there are obvious problems with this situation, especially because your teen, unlike a real spy, has emotional ties to both countries (parents), meaning that when either parent asks for information and we give it, we feel like we're stabbing the other parent in the back. We know that you want to know what is going on at your ex-spouse's home, but you are forcing us into an incredibly uncomfortable position. We know you're curious and feel like we have to tell you what you want to know. But at the same time we feel like turncoats, going back and forth, giving classified information to the other side.

DATING, AGAIN

I hated it when my mom would date, probably because it was weird for me that she was going to be with anyone other than my dad. So when she would bring guys home, I would do everything I could possibly do to make sure that he knew I hated him. Normally this process would consist of me giving the guy a battery of questions, all of which he of course had the wrong answers to. I would ask him his job, age, if he had children, his plans for the future, his religion, how long he has been single, and on and on. I covered basically everything other than shoe size and pant length, much to my mother's dismay.

I recently asked my mom what she did about this because she never really said anything to me other than the occasional, "Shut up!" She informed me that before she would bring anyone to meet me, she would have to give him her warning speech. Looking back on it, my battery of questions was probably not the nicest thing in the world to do, but even now things have not changed too much. I still tend to quiz my mom's dates, but I'm trying to be more understanding. Although not too long ago my mom brought home a guy who, under my interrogation, revealed himself to be a Unitarian. He explained that his religion accepts the beliefs of all people, which I took as an easy opening. Just as I was getting warmed up on my classic fail-safe "What about Hitler . . ." argument, Mom stepped in.

Maybe that was in bad taste, but the thing is, it is very hard for us when a parent starts to date. Because we feel that you should not be doing it, we will find a way to hate whomever you are going to bring home way before you actually do. Like typical teens, we will make sure you know this—

or even worse, make sure your date knows this. Still, teens have told me there are some things you can do that will make your dating sit just a little bit better with us.

"I think it's weird that you'd want to date again."

> *My mom and dad have been divorced for 2 years, and my dad is starting to go out again. I did not like the whole idea, and I told him that. He asked me why, and I told him that it just made me feel weird. He said that he understood that I did not like him dating, but it had been a long time since he and my mom got divorced, and he needed to move on. He said that we were a family and that he wanted my support in this whole thing. He told me that it was just as weird for him as it was for me that he was dating again. I understood what he was saying, and even though I still thought that it was weird, I got eventually over it because I knew he felt the same way I did.*
>
> JOANNA, AGE 14, TALIHINA, OKLAHOMA

By fully opening up to Joanna and telling her exactly what he was feeling, her dad helped her to understand where he was coming from. Many teens have told me that by being truthful and honest, you have a better chance at making us feel better about you dating again, and you also have a better chance at keeping those dates. (Sorry, Mom!)

"I can't believe you actually like him!"

I think it's fair to say that not every date you bring home is going to be welcomed with a ticker-tape parade by your teen. And as long as you're not really into them that much, maybe that's okay. But what about when your teen dislikes somebody you really *do* like?

> ***My mom is dating this guy who I hate. She keeps on telling me to give him a chance, and I truthfully do, but I still hate him. Well, no matter how many times I tell her that I do not like him, she still goes out with him. If she doesn't care what I think, then she shouldn't ask me.***
>
> SAM, AGE 15, OVETT, MISSISSIPPI

What Sam said, as easy as it sounds, is one solution to this problem. Teens have told me that they would like you to take their advice when picking people to date, but if you are not willing to do that, they want you to tell them that. Because if what we say will not make a difference, then there is no use for us to complain to you about how much we do not like this or that about this or that person. On the other hand, if you decide that you will take into account what we say and we happen to dislike the person that you are dating, ask us why we feel the way we do. When we give you our reasons, we want to be heard (not just brushed off with a "You don't know what she's really like speech"). Plus, that way you can work on possibly changing our minds. (Good luck on that one.)

"I feel uncomfortable calling you Dad."

One of the biggest problems that I had with the person who became my stepdad was the fact that he wanted me to call him Dad. I did not want to hurt him by not calling him Dad because I knew that he wanted it so bad, so I tried my best at it. I spoke to my mom and she agreed that I should try because it would make him feel better. I called him Dad for a while, but it just sounded too unnatural coming from my mouth; I already had a dad, so it was weird giving someone else his title.

When my dad got remarried, my stepmom, whom I liked, wanted me to call her Mom. I knew how much she wanted me to do this, so as much as I didn't want to, I did. Not only did it make her happy, it also made my dad happy because she was happy. So everyone was happy except for me. And even though I wanted to stop calling her Mom after a while, I couldn't because then she would know I was calling her Mom this whole time and never meaning it, something that would have killed her. I've called her Mom ever since, and it pains me every time—not only because she isn't my mom, but be-

cause I'm resentful that I was made to call her that in the first place.

MOLLY, AGE 18, RANDOR, OHIO

While few stepparents will *demand* that their stepkids call them Mom or Dad, teens have told me that just by *asking* them to do this, you could unintentionally be putting a guilt trip on them. We realize how happy this would make you feel, and it's not that we don't want you to be happy, but titles like Mom and Dad are emotionally charged, especially if the teen's biological mom or dad is still in the picture. The teens I've spoken with say that the best thing to do in this situation is to let us decide what to call you. And maybe, when the time is right, we'll be thrilled to call you by the name you've always wanted to hear.

Cracking the Code:

A Mom's View on What a Parent Can Do

When my second marriage broke up, Kyle was just entering her teen years, and Rhett was still a little younger. The breakup didn't happen overnight, and I know the kids did hear us fight occasionally, but that wasn't the biggest problem.

The biggest problem was that it was hard for me to realize that the kids needed to deal with the situation in their own ways. Kyle, especially, wanted the opportunity to sit down with Ralph after he had left to talk to him and get some closure of her own.

I honestly didn't understand. I was trying to protect my kids from the harsh realities of life, and the way I came across was, "I've got my closure, why isn't that good enough for you?"

This became one of the real learning experiences of my life as a parent. I had to learn to understand that my closure wasn't enough. Kyle wasn't being disloyal to me by wanting to talk to Ralph; she just needed to work through her own issues to get her own closure. Divorce is a painful experience for everyone, and everyone's pain is different, and personal.

When it comes to this issue, in a very powerful way, we need to listen to our kids, because on this subject they really do know more than we do about what they're going through.

One of the things that came through loud and clear from the teens Rhett spoke with is that they really feel the pain that comes from their parents' arguments. Nothing's as heartbreaking as this, and nothing hits home as hard. In other chapters of Rhett's book, we've had to confront the question, "What can we, as parents, do to help our teenage kids?" In this chapter, the question is "What are we, as parents, doing to hurt our kids?"

Here's one quote that haunts me, from Jess in Kansas:

"Every time I try to talk to my parents about their fighting, they always tell me not to worry about it because it has nothing to do with me. But I think it does."

How do I respond to that? I know, instinctively, that Jess shouldn't feel that, and that I—that we parents—have to find a way to get through to her that she shouldn't feel that.

Anthony Gribin, Ph.D., in private practice in Morristown, New Jersey, told me this: "Kids are never the subject of the fight. Neither is sex, and neither is money. Those are things that people argue about, but they aren't the real subject, which is the inability to compromise."

For that reason, Dr. Gribin pointed out, we need to really examine this issue of arguing in front of the kids. Rhett's respondents all agreed that it's the worst thing you can do. But when they think of arguments, they think of the arguments that hurt the most.

It's important to remember that arguments are a part of every relationship, but that not every argument is the first step toward divorce.

"If kids see that there can be a resolution to conflict—that there's an actual outcome—then it can be healthy for them to see parents arguing," Dr. Gribin points out.

We don't want our kids to think that every argument is the first step on the road to disaster. They don't have to think that arguments have to be avoided at all costs, and they don't have to think that total annihilation of the other person is the successful outcome of an argument. To the extent that they see healthy arguments can result in a healthy resolution, this can be a real learning experience.

"But on the other hand," Dr. Gribin says, "if parents know they're heading for divorce, they shouldn't argue in front of the kids, because then kids will see arguments without resolution."

How do you know you're heading for divorce? Most of us don't. We don't want to give up on our marriages, and we don't want to get divorced. But there are still things we can ask ourselves. Are our arguments changing in tone? Are they changing in frequency? Are we arguing more than we used to? Do our arguments end in a feeling of futility or bitterness? These types of arguments should not take place when the kids can hear them.

Not surprisingly, these types of arguments are the hardest to control. How do we stop them from happening in front of the kids?

I'm not going to give a simple formula answer to this question. But I will say this. It's something we all know, but it can't be repeated too often. *Parenting is a full-time job.* Even if you're heading toward a point where you won't be a wife anymore, or you won't be a husband anymore, you're still a parent, and you're still going to be a parent. Remember that being a parent comes first.

What do you do if your kids *do* hear you fighting about them? Or if they hear you fighting, and they think it's about them?

Saying "it's not about you, honey," isn't enough. So what is? Many of Rhett's respondents say, "we want to know everything." Others got to know everything and discovered it was too much.

No one can ever know everything. Jane Austen said it best: "Seldom, very seldom, does complete truth belong to any human disclosure." If we try to tell everything, no matter how fair we try to be, we're only telling our side of everything.

Here's what I think. Give them Dr. Gribin's analysis. Teens so often say, as we've read throughout this book, "don't personalize." Well, here's a place where it may be really good not to personalize. Don't say, "it's not about you, honey." Say, "Kids are *never* the subject of the fight." And explain what that means. "People—not your mom and your dad, but all people—when they have arguments that can't be resolved are expressing their inability to compromise. They're expressing that they are fundamentally too different to find a middle ground."

If your teen angrily tells you, "Well, *find* a way to compromise! That's your job! You're my parents!" at least the anger is not misplaced, and not turned inward. And the teen is probably right. It is a parent's job. But we can't always do that job. And anger that's expressed, and expressed in a valid way, can lead somewhere. It can be the beginning of communication.

I don't have all the answers here. There's more than enough pain to go around in any divorce. But we do know that parenting means communication, and we know that it's ultimately our job as parents—with all the help we can get, from Rhett and his respondents, from our own teens, from experts—to make that communication work.

If the arguing and fighting with your ex-spouse isn't bad enough for your kids, then the other shoe drops: dating someone new.

Here's a story one of my friends told me.

"After my husband left, and after the shock had subsided a little, I noticed something interesting: Communication with my two teenage daughters was actually improving. For one thing, our house became a comfortable place for teenagers and their friends to congregate. My husband had always made it sort of uncomfortable for them.

"Things started to get relaxed and a lot more fun. One day, my girls and a couple of their friends were hanging out, and my 16-year-old daughter said, 'Mom, it's time that you started dating again. We need to prepare a list of questions so we can interview your prospective dates. Let's see. . . .'

"That's when my 17-year-old broke in: 'What brand of condoms do you use?'

"That was the end of the list-making, as everyone collapsed in a fit of giggles. But my wonderful daughters—in front of their friends—had made their point. Not that they expected me to start having sex with other men, or that they would really interview guys about condoms. But that they understood what I was going through, and that they'd be supportive of me."

Humor helps any situation. If you can joke with your kids—and that doesn't mean make fun of your kids—you can open up a lot of doors of communication.

In the issue of dating and possible remarriage, we run up against the same paradox as before. Kids want to know everything; they don't want to feel left out. But they don't really want to know everything. Not everything is their business, all knowledge is half-knowledge, and some knowledge can hurt. A lot. And unnecessarily.

Dr. Gribin says, "Don't bring someone home unless the relationship is really solid. In fact, don't even let the kids know you're dating someone specific until he seems like a real possibility. Then you can say, well, I met this nice guy, we're going to the movies tonight. Don't bring him home until the kids start asking, when are we going to meet So-and-so? Then bring him home, but make it short and sweet. Don't start by inviting him for dinner. Eating dinner with Mom's new guy is a very intense time. Move the relationship along as gradually as possible.

"Before that, they don't have to know that you're dating. If you start going out with friends, having a social life, you don't need to supply any details. If your friends fix you up with one guy this week, and another guy next week, and you have coffee or dinner but nothing comes of it, your kids don't have to know that at all."

But then what happens if things are going well and you introduce someone to your kids—and it doesn't go well? What about the situation where your kids hate the new guy, or the new woman? The first thing to do is find out why they hate him. And is it hate, or is it a problem that can be worked out?

A good way to start: Ask. Find out if there are problems that can be resolved. Are there things the new guy is actually doing that rub your teens the wrong way? Or would they just hate anyone you started dating? If it's the former, then New Guy needs to be brought into the discussion. If it's the latter, then you and your kids have to work it out.

Sam from Mississippi says, "No matter how many times I tell my mom that I do not like him she *still* goes out with him. If she doesn't care what I think, then she shouldn't ask me."

But I think there's a middle ground there, too. I think you need to let your kids know that their opinion does matter, their feelings do matter, and that you'll work with them to make the situation better, but that they can't control your life. Teens are moving toward independence, toward controlling their own lives. You can control your own life, and still be part of a family, with respect and communication.

RESOURCES

Abuse

National Domestic Violence Hotline (NDVH)
PO Box 161810
Austin, TX 78716
(800) 799-SAFE
(800) 799-7233
(800) 787-3224
E-mail ndvh@ndvh.org
www.ndvh.org

You can e-mail questions and concerns to NDVH or find more information on their Web site about domestic violence abuse.

Child Welfare League of America
440 First Street, NW, Third Floor
Washington, DC 20001-2085
(202) 638-2952
www.cwla.org

The Child Welfare League of America is the oldest and largest membership based child welfare organization, committed to promoting the well-being of children and families.

Childhelp USA
(800) 4 A CHILD
www.childhelpusa.org

Childhelp USA exists to meet the physical, emotional, educational, and spiritual needs of abused and neglected children.

Broken Families

Rainbows
2100 Golf Road, #370
Rolling Meadows, IL 60008
(800) 266-3206
(847) 952-1770
E-mail info@rainbows.org
www.rainbows.org

This organization fosters emotional healing among children who are grieving a loss from a life-altering crisis. It offers good information on dealing with death and divorce.

About.com
http://parentingteens.about.com/cs/divorceteens

About.com offers many links to articles and websites that can help parents get children and teens through the divorce.

Diet and Eating Disorders

TeensHealth
http://kidshealth.org/teen/food_fitness
This site provides a wide variety of information on dieting, fad supplements (including steroids), exercise, and eating disorders. It also offers lots of other useful information for kids, teens, and parents on things ranging from general health to emotional health.

National Eating Disorders Association
603 Stewart Street, Suite 803
Seattle, WA 98101
(206) 382-3587
E-mail info@NationalEatingDisorders.org
www.nationaleatingdisorders.org
This site offers information about the different types of eating disorders and their causes, treatment, and prevention.

U.S. Food and Drug Adminstration (FDA)
(800) INFO-FDA
www.fda.gov/opacom/7teens.html
The FDA periodically reprints articles with important teen health information in their "Teen Scene" section.

Gay Issues

The Gay & Lesbian Alliance Against Defamation (GLAAD)
5455 Wilshire Boulevard, Suite 1500
Los Angeles, CA 90036
(323) 933-2240
248 West 35th Street, 8th Floor
New York, NY 10001
(212) 629-3322
www.glaad.org
GLAAD is dedicated to promoting and ensuring fair, accurate, and inclusive representation of people and events in the media as a means of eliminating homophobia and discrimination based on gender identity and sexual orientation.

Gayteens Resources
www.gayteens.org
www.healthyplace.com/communities/gender/gayisok

Money

***Money Still Doesn't Grow on Trees: A Parent's Guide to Raising Financially Responsible Teens and Young Adults*, by Neale S. Godfrey**
A comprehensive approach to helping parents teach budgeting, smart spending, the work ethic, and financial decision making. Available in bookstores and through www.Rodale.com

Sex

The Sex Education Coalition
6101 Wilson Lane
Bethesda, MD 20817
www.sexedcoalition.org

The SEC has a very complete section of links to sites where teens can ask questions about sexuality, find sex education resources, or discuss sex issues responsibly with other teens.

The Sexuality Information and Education Council of the U.S. (SIECUS)
130 W. 42nd Street, #350
New York, NY 10036
(212) 819-9770
E-mail siecus@siecus.org
www.siecus.org

SIECUS is a national, nonprofit organization that affirms sexuality is a natural and healthy part of living. Incorporated in 1964, SIECUS develops, collects, and disseminates information; promotes comprehensive education about sexuality; and advocates the right of individuals to make responsible sexual choices.

Planned Parenthood Federation of America
434 West 33rd Street
New York, NY 10001
(212) 541-7800
www.plannedparenthood.org

Planned Parenthood Federation of America is the world's largest and most trusted voluntary reproductive health care organization. Planned Parenthood believes in everyone's right to choose whether or when to have a child, that every child should be wanted and loved, and that women should be in charge of their own destinies. Planned Parenthood's teenager site, http://teenwire.com, answers questions about sexual health.

Scarleteen
www.scarleteen.com

Scarleteen feels that the best model for lifelong sexual education is as follows: providing information that educates in ALL aspects of positive sexuality.

Substance Abuse

National Institute on Drug Abuse (NIDA)
National Institutes of Health
6001 Executive Boulevard, Room 5213
Bethesda, MD 20892-9561
(301) 443-1124
www.drugabuse.gov/NIDAHome.html

They have an excellent list of drugs, their street names, their effects and possible dangers at www.nida.nih.gov/DrugsofAbuse.html.

Focus Adolescent Services
(410) 341-4342
(877) 362-8727
E-mail focusashelp@aol.com
www.focusas.com/
SubstanceAbuse.html

The Focus Web site has information on drug, tobacco, and alcohol abuse with a lot of useful facts and links.

Freevibe
http://freevibe.com

Freevibe features facts on drugs, personal stories from teens, and ways to avoid peer pressure.

Suicide

American Academy of Pediatrics
141 Northwest Point Boulevard
Elk Grove Village, IL 60007-1098
(847) 434-4000
www.aap.org/visit/suicideinfo.htm

Check this site for good information for parents on signs, prevention, and coping with depression and suicide attempts.

Child Suicide
http://childsuicide.homestead.com/
HelpforTeens.html

This site offers a variety of links to help kids and teens work through feelings of depression or thoughts of suicide.

Tattoos and Body Piercing

TeensHealth
www.kidshealth.org/teen/question/
skin/body_piercing_safe.html
Go here for good information on all the negatives about tattoos and piercing, followed by some sound information on doing it safely.

General Sites for Teens

About.com
www.teenadvice.about.com

This Web site offers information, quizzes, facts, and advice on a wide array of subjects pertinent to teenagers.

Youth Source
www.youthsource.cc

Youth Source has monthly topics, ranging from drugs, alcohol, suicide, and abuse.